Mr.
PLANNING
COMMISSIONER

By HAROLD V. MILLER

Executive Director
Tennessee State Planning Commission

PUBLIC ADMINISTRATION SERVICE

1954

NA
9030
.M5

DEDICATION

This little book is dedicated to the thousands of men and women who give of their time, their wisdom and their hearts in selfless, unpaid service through membership on local planning commissions; especially to those who have recently been appointed to the planning commission in their home community and to those who will succeed those now serving.

FOREWORD

Across the country in great cities, small towns and rural counties, thousands of men and women contribute time and thought as members of local planning commissions. Almost without exception, no salary is paid for this great service.

Persons willing to undertake such responsibilities should be helped as much as possible to obtain as soon as possible an understanding of the field of planning and of their powers and responsibilities as planning commissioners. This book was written in an effort to provide such help.

This is not a classroom textbook in planning. There are a number of such in existence.

This is not a scholarly summary of the finest examples of official planning to date.

This is in the form of a discourse presented as it were to the newly appointed member of a recently established planning commission in a town of medium size. It is believed that many of the principles set forth herein will be applicable or adaptable to other planning undertakings whether the commission be new or well established and whether the community be large or small.

TABLE OF CONTENTS

I

SO YOU'RE THE NEW
PLANNING COMMISSIONER?

Mr. Commissioner! Oh, Mr. Commissioner! You *are* Mr. Jones, the new member of the planning commission here, aren't you? I've been anxious to meet you and to tell you how glad I am that you have accepted the mayor's appointment to the planning commission.

I understand that you were quite surprised at the suggestion that you become a member of the commission; that you were rather reticent about accepting the appointment. You are needed for the job, though, and well suited to the task. I know that you may not have had specialized training in the field of planning and that you may not have held public office before, but those are not really prerequisites. There are approximately 15,000 to 20,000 citizens across the country who are serving as members of local planning commissions; many of them are just like you. Very, very few of them had any training in or professional relationships to local planning programs when they were asked by the mayor or city manager to serve on the planning commission.

They, like you, probably said, "But why appoint me? I'm no planner. I've never held public office. I'm a busy man. I try to take my share of church work and keep up with the projects of the civic club. I vote, pay my taxes and all that sort of thing, but as far as holding public office is concerned — well, I never thought of it. Why don't you find somebody else?" He probably came right back and said, "We know all that, but I believe you're the man we want. You've got a good reputation in the community, you've been fair in your dealings with your neighbors. You've got your roots down in this town and you're interested in its future. You've got three fine kids coming along, and you want it to be a good place for them to grow up and settle in. So don't tell me 'no' because I really want to appoint you to fill this vacancy."

Thousands of citizens have been recruited in much this same way and put to work on planning commissions without pay all across the country. You may think this a rather slip-shod method of recruiting: a local chief official exercising his appointive powers and hunting around and finding somebody who's willing to serve for nothing on a local planning commission. It really isn't slip-shod. It's one of the finest things in modern American government, and it really is something when good citizens are willing to serve their communities in this manner, especially in these days when it seems like so many people will do nothing at all for anybody unless they get paid plenty for doing it. That American trait just tends to highlight the service on local planning commissions as one of the finer aspects of democracy in action.

Mr. Commissioner, I have no other arrangements for lunch. Why don't we have lunch together and perhaps we could chat a bit about where your planning commission fits into the machinery of government of which it is an official branch?

II

AN IMPORTANT MAN IN LOCAL GOVERNMENT

Where does the planning commissioner fit into the structure of government?

Well,' let's back off a bit and take the longer look at the whole situation and gradually work right up to your position.

I suppose that we could say that there has always been planning. People have planned ever since the first human being decided to live in a cave where he would be protected from the weather, would have solid rock on three sides of him and would only have to mind the fourth side in watching out for the approach of his enemies.

As we come down through history, men began to live in groups — I don't know just when they began to call them cities. Certainly the medieval cities showed a kind of planning, for they were compact areas full of people and surrounded by a high wall that helped in the defense of the group and prevented complete surprise by the enemies.

Later, in this country, the laying out of the village Commons in New England and the drafting of a system of streets for Washington, D. C., by Major L'Enfant were examples of a kind of planning having a visual, physical expression in the community.

During the latter part of the last century our bigger, older cities began to suffer from too-narrow streets, mixtures of buildings, and other difficulties. Because these circumstances led to what we think of as city planning, now practiced in large and small places alike, let's take a quick look at what went on.

In the latter part of the last century, Olmsted came forward with a plan for Central Park in New York City and in a sense started a cycle of park planning. Also, tenement conditions in New York City festered to the point where a civic consciousness was aroused and it was realized that community action was necessary. Tenement house laws resulted.

Then came the Chicago World's Fair of 1893 and men and women from all over the country first saw the aesthetic and utilitarian possibilities of an orderly arrangement of monumental buildings, roads and grounds. Almost immediately the "City Beautiful" movement got under way across the country with emphasis on monumental buildings, boulevards and formal landscaping.

Meanwhile, cities were growing by leaps and bounds and, because of the increase in the number of people, there were all sorts of problems. The quiet little streets which more or less adequately served the original settlements became crowded even with the horse-drawn vehicles of the day. As water needs increased and local ground water

3

became polluted, the individual or neighborhood wells were abandoned and central water and sewer systems were substituted. These were expensive advances. However, land values were increasing and with elevators, buildings could be built higher and higher on individual lots. City planning of a sort was undertaken and found its primary expression in the widening of streets. These increased land values, however, had a dampening effect on street widening because costs increased so much.

The advent of the automobile and rapid transit lines in larger cities made possible the escape from the highly crowded areas of some of the people who had the money, inclination and time to move to suburbs where they could have more trees, more space, and more pleasant surroundings for their homes and families. But the automobile and rapid transit also made possible more people working and shopping in the central areas of the cities, and congestion continued to mount.

A few farsighted leaders were giving serious thought to some of the underlying causes of the situation and in so doing might well have summarized the situation something like this:

So the city has a police department and the policemen, to a reasonably satisfactory degree, bring to justice those who have acted wrongly in the eyes of society. At the same time, there is a great deal of expense involved directly and indirectly in simply bearing down on the wrongdoers after-the-fact. How much better if the incidence of crime could be cut down; and there must be some reason why crime is more prevalent and a greater percentage of the population has a criminal record in some sections of the city than in other sections.

Again, there are the engineers who apply their professional skills in the building of water plants and extending water mains into those sections of the city crying for service, and they do a pretty good job. Yet, there is one thing that always plagues them and that is the question of where and how much water is going to be needed. Such information would permit them to lay the right size pipes in the first place — not find their pipes outgrown and have to lay new ones. Or, if they err in the other direction, they find that they had used their available money in laying short stretches of unnecessarily large and unnecessarily expensive pipe.

Other engineers work on sewers and streets. They lay sewers that will drain all right, and devise new types of pavement that will give more miles of all-weather surface for the money available for streets at a particular time. But some of the sewers have turned out to be too small for the ultimate load and others have turned out to be larger than would have been necessary if someone had looked ahead. Similarly, some of the streets were built extra heavy, at great expense, for traffic which never materialized, and other streets built in a low-cost manner for residential service have been broken up by heavy traffic, and houses along these streets have become less desirable to live in because of the passage of many vehicles, including heavy trucks.

The fire department is manned with alert and well-trained personnel so that they are able to put out fires in a manner that is above reproach. But in many instances it has been difficult to get back between the buildings to go to work on the fire. Also, many buildings were so constructed that fire could spread easily from one building to another.

Schools have become increasingly important. Some of them have been located in areas in which, since the population has shifted, very few children live and thus pupils have to travel long distances to get to school. Others have been located on relatively small lots, and, having been added to from time to time, cover the whole lot leaving no play space and no opportunity to maintain grounds and plants which would shield the school from street noises.

Then there are those things which too often happen directly in connection with the places where people live. When the average citizen puts his life savings and perhaps obligates himself for payments for the next twenty years on a home of his own, he may find his property values destroyed. Someone may build right up to the property line next to him and destroy the looks of his place. Or, he may find that when he wants to sell his house he can't get much for it because very few people care to live next to a repair garage or some all-night joint, or junk yard, or a factory of some sort.

These were some of the considerations which led in the early twenties to a more general recognition that there is a better way to develop a city than just to run a police department and a fire department and a school department and a street department; there was a wiser recourse than to trust to luck that property values will not be destroyed, and that the community, by the grace of God and through the unrelated efforts of everybody concerned would grow into and remain a pleasant, efficient and economically sound place to live, to do business and to invest your money. Farsighted leaders began to visualize the working together of all of these and other forces contributing to civic development according to an agreed upon general plan with each knowing what the other is doing and what might be expected in the future.

Volunteer citizens' committees were established here and there and, for the most part, these were manned and financed by business and professional men who contributed money and talent in an effort to guide and direct the growth of their home communities. These efforts served a very beneficial effect, for they pioneered in the development of community-wide plans and also led to exploration of legal bases for putting some of the plans into effect.

In the late 1920's a number of the states, acting on the basis of these pioneering efforts passed enabling legislation which would permit cities by appropriate ordinance to establish *official* planning commissions. The enabling legislation in most instances granted fairly wide powers to such local planning commissions so that they really had authority and legal tools to use in making and carrying out plans for their cities. These plans, as we will note a little later on, could involve a considerable variety of subject matter and thus constructively touch and guide a wide variety of conditions and phases of the community.

Now these local planning commissions were not super-governments imposed on the existing and traditional government with its various departments; they did not take over the police activities and they did not actually build the new streets. The planning commission occupied, insofar as possible, a non-partisan position in city government. It was legally set up as a branch of city government and, in most of their work, they were advisory to the duly elected officials of city government. There are only a few things, such as subdivision regulations, on which they had the final word, but if their viewpoint was comprehensive and their advice sound, then their position, even though advisory, could be and still is of tremendous importance in the community's affairs and in charting the community's future.

So, Mr. Commissioner, your office is relatively new in the American scene. While you cannot trace your professional ancestry back through thousands of years, as do the doctors to Hippocrates, you nevertheless in a very real sense hold the future of your children, your neighbors and your city in the hollow of your hand. It is largely up to you what view you take of your office. You could take a narrow view and simply appear as a referee or once in a while make some decisions to help the elected administration get off a hot spot. How different it will be if you choose to work really systematically and intelligently and *do a job* of planning for your city! Though planning techniques now available to you were in large part developed in the larger, older cities, you can apply them in smaller or newer places, guide your growth and avoid trouble.

6

The cards are stacked in your favor in that you come to your position of Planning Commissioner without partisan political label and untrammeled by election promises. You are in a position to exercise your very best judgment and foresight and to do so fearlessly, for you are not dependent on this job for a livelihood. You can always look your neighbors, singly or collectively, in the eye and say with conviction, "This is my best judgment on the matter."

You are indeed in a strategic position. Nevertheless, you have the very real moral obligation to analyze your powers and responsibilities as well as the techniques at your disposal for doing the job, and then *do* it in such a manner that both your contemporaries and those yet to come will favorably remember you as an important man in local government.

III

THE GENERAL PROPOSITION

Too few planning commission members find or make the opportunity to discuss all their powers and duties and to gain some sort of over-all view of the field of planning. In far too many instances, the commission member simply attends meetings, gives serious consideration to whatever items happen to be brought to his attention, and maybe he serves on committees of the commission giving special study to specific subjects.

Too often the commission member fails to sense the ramifications of his actions. Often he does not see clearly how what he does here will have an influence on something over there. It's rather like the small boy going down the sidewalk and brushing against a good, tight, well-clipped hedge. Even if he bumps into only one part of the hedge, you'll notice a sort of shock wave that travels from bush to bush and branch to branch until there's at least a small vibration in the other end of the hedge after a moment or two.

It's much the same way in connection with planning decisions. Let's take a concrete example. You decide that a particular street ought to be widened or that as it is extended it should be laid out to a good generous width for you have in mind that it should be a major street in that part of town. This may be entirely warranted and a very fine step, but you soon realize that this major street is not an isolated fact. By virtue of its generous width and good alignment it soon becomes a popular channel over which a considerable volume of traffic will move. You will soon find individuals coming up with the idea of establishing businesses along that street because they feel that the heavy traffic would automatically make this frontage a good place for business. The street will also give better access to an undeveloped section of the city and the owners of the land begin to take an interest in subdividing. As lots are sold, residences begin to spring up. These, in turn, will call for new or enlarged schools in that area. Similarly, the pattern of needs and facilities will be altered in terms of demands for water, sewer services and bus service. Perhaps the town will grow enough in that direction so that a new fire station needs to be set up. Still other items could be mentioned, but there's no point in taking time on those right now because *any* new development of any consequence will lead to still further change. Thus, it is of the utmost importance that major steps be taken in accord with a well-formulated plan, a plan that anticipates the consequences which will follow. For example, the opening of the major street without the recognition of the ensuing need for water and sewer service could mean that the street would be paved and then the pavement would have to be chopped up within a few months or a year or two to install the water and sewer lines. It is obvious to both of us that this would be silly, short-sighted and involve a needless expenditure of public funds, but just stop and think how often in your own experience you have seen this happen.

Yes, the field of planning looks complicated and especially so to a new commissioner, but we can strip it down to its essentials, take its measure and go on from there. David Lilienthal, who in other years headed the Tennessee Valley Authority and then the Atomic Energy Commission, had an almost uncanny ability to size up a knotty situation and strip it down to the bare essentials. He would then make his decisions on the basis of those essentials and was in a position to relate the details and ramifications back to his decisions, just like hanging ornaments on a Christmas tree. Let's try the same approach in considering the general proposition of planning.

In the first place, the people who set up your planning commission were not primarily motivated by a desire for *plans*. They recognized the need for *action*. And for that action to be intelligent, it would be necessary to have plans on which to act. That's where you come in.

Realizing that every significant thing that you do will have ramifying effects throughout the community, your real need is for a comprehensive plan for your community as soon as possible. You will find some folks speaking of this as the "Master Plan," but the chances are they will mean the same thing I do when I say Comprehensive Plan. I like my terminology better, because psychologically there is something so final and so static conjured up by the words, Master Plan. Actually, the further you go and the more your community grows, the clearer you will see that no plan can be final and that no plan worth having should be allowed to remain static.

In the simplest sense your comprehensive plan should contain two major groups of ideas. The first group of ideas will relate to the *use of land* throughout your area of jurisdiction, and the second group of ideas will pertain to *services* to the various portions of your area and to the users of the land.

Let's look at it this way. Our bodies have their various members and organs. We function properly only when we have all of these various parts. Similarly, normal cities cannot grow soundly unless the parts are all provided, and unless there are spaces for living, places for work, areas for recreation, business areas and means of circulation between them. And what is more, there are organic relationships between these various kinds of land use appearing in various parts of the city.

To be at all realistic, the land use plan will normally reflect to

9

some extent the existing uses of land, but inasmuch as the plan looks to the future it may well include some changes that ought to be made as and when possible. It should indicate areas into which the various uses should be guided and provided for — housing, industrial areas, schools, parks and playgrounds, central and local service business areas, and space for transportation and circulation.

The services and facilities planning will embrace all of those items that the community has decided should be provided for its inhabitants through common rather than individual action. Thus these will include streets, transit facilities, public buildings, water, electricity and sewers, together with fire, recreation and other facilities.

It should be obvious that there is a strong interrelationship between the *land use plan effectuation* and the *services and facilities plan effectuation*. It is true that the distribution of population will have a strong effect on the need for services. At the same time, the availability or non-availability of services will go a long way toward determining the distribution of population, since this affects the attractiveness of given areas as the scene of residential, industrial or other development.

If you don't mind, sir, let me toss in at this point several other items which you ought to check up on and be sure just where you stand before you get very far into the planning process.

First, you should check pertinent legislation to understand clearly and exactly what your powers and responsibilities are, both in terms of the city ordinance which set up your planning commission, and the state legislation which authorizes the cities to establish planning commissions and grant them powers. You will want to know just what your obligations are in order that you may fulfill them better. You will also want to know what powers are at your disposal — in other words, the legal tools which make up your working kit.

You would also want to check the matter of organization. Be sure that the requirements of law have been fulfilled. For instance, do you have the right number of members on the planning commission as may be specified by law? Has the planning commission organized itself by electing one of its members chairman and by electing such other officers from among its number as may be required? Furthermore, is it clearly understood just where you fit into city government — do you report to the chief executive or the legislative body? Be sure you know where you fit in.

You will want to look over your fellow commissioners. Get to know them. Find out their interests and talents. You might be interested in knowing whether they afford reasonable geographic representation of the various parts of the city. You will wish to know who of them is serving in an ex-officio capacity, that is, by virtue of his being a member of the executive or legislative branch of city government and who will be a valuable liaison man with city government. But above all, you will want to find out whether your fellow commissioners have a real interest in their job, whether they can see the whole city and feel its needs and potentialities and whether they share your enthusiasm over helping to see that every new building erected and every improvement undertaken makes its full contribution toward the improvement of your city.

Yes, Mr. Commissioner, you've got a big job ahead of you, particularly if you want to use this opportunity and this new position to make a real and lasting contribution to the development of your town.

IV

GETTING STARTED

Well, Mr. Commissioner, I hope that we haven't gotten you so involved in general considerations that you have begun to feel like the whole business is a big formless mess about which you could do nothing. I certainly wouldn't want you to feel like one local planning commission member did when he said to me, "You know, up to a certain point and as I learned how much there was to planning, I began to feel like I was trying to pick up several hundred pounds of loose cotton all at one time and toss it into a truck. It just seemed like I couldn't get hold of the thing. There just weren't any handles on it!"

Now that you are convinced that there is something there, let's do our best to put some handles on it so that you can get a good firm grip anywhere that you choose to start.

In speaking of where you should choose to start, let me make this one suggestion. I wish you'd see if you can find out just why your planning commission was established. If it was established very recently, it should not be too difficult to find the stimulus. Oh, the cause might be any of several things. I recall one planning commission which was established within a matter of a few days after a filling station went under construction next door to the banker's house and, believe me, the banker did quite a job of convincing the mayor that the town needed a planning commission so that it could work toward setting up a good zoning ordinance and plan for the town.

In other places there were other reasons. In one town which called me in some years ago they wanted plans for a system of major streets and (for the moment at least) they didn't particularly care whether or not there were any plans drafted for other aspects of the community. It so happened that a young doctor had come to town and he pointed out that the only way to get from one side of the railroad to the other was by one of three grade crossings which could all be blocked by trains at the same time. The townspeople began to get scared, wondering how they could get the fire engine or the ambulance across from where it was to where it ought to be.

Again, a sizeable industry had located a mile or two outside another town. The influx of construction workers led to unprecedented traffic jams and parking difficulties. These circumstances drove home to the local people a realization that their planning, especially for traffic and parking, was long overdue.

But why should I bring up the question of why your planning commission was established when you are expecting a nice neat answer as to how to get started on your planning?

In the first place, maybe I can't give such a nice neat answer. And in the second place, a sober analysis of your particular situation might suggest accelerated attention to some specific phase of the planning program that the people want to have attended to first. If so, get at it if at all feasible. You will win friends and gain community support if you can find answers to those problems that are plaguing the population most. You can well use that support through the years if you are going to carry out your plans in the American tradition of public support and democratic decision — not action by edict.

Proceed soundly, though. If you toss out offhand opinions like sparks off a pinwheel, good and bad suggestions alike will soon be ignored. Be sure you've got something worth saying.

I strongly contend that there is an ideal way to go about planning for a community. At the same time, I would be the first to acknowledge that carrying through with the ideal procedure and development of a comprehensive plan may well take several years. Even then, there should follow a continuing process of further planning and adaptation throughout the years.

Now, if in the pursuit of the ideal, so much time is consumed that the immediate needs of the community are not met, almost inevitably there will be a slacking off of public interest and the planning effort may die. If that happens, planning may be very difficult to resurrect. So work with these interested citizens on the problem that is of interest to them and show them a logical solution and, in turn, they will stand behind you as you proceed more deliberately and thoroughly with the development and execution of your general plan.

In any case, and regardless of the questions that you tackle first, you are going to need maps. Actually you'll need maps at almost every step of your program and you really should make them early and use them constantly. You'll need them in order to tell you the things you need to know in order to make decisions, and you'll need still more maps on which to record your decisions. Normally, these maps will cover the city which is your area of jurisdiction, but occasionally you'll need a map showing the city in relation to its surrounding region. And from time to time you'll want to be using maps covering only parts of your city but probably showing it in greater detail.

I really mean it when I say you should use maps just about all the time in your planning program. The planning, to be sound, must comprehend the entire community, the relation of its various parts and the distribution of things in the community. Sure, I know, you've lived here until you feel like you know the old town like the palm of your hand. But I venture to say there's still ample opportunity for you to learn more about the town and you'd probably be genuinely surprised at some of the things that will show up on a good series of maps.

I really mean it, too, when I say that much of the results of your planning must or should be displayed on maps. If you say to folks that Elm Street should be widened from Third to Tenth avenues, they may mildly agree with you. Or they might feel that it is one of those ideas sprung out from under the table in a smoke-filled room. If, on the other hand, you have your maps showing the traffic situation and how traffic movement would be expedited by the widening of Elm Street from Third to Tenth and showing where Elm Street fits into a circulation system for the community, then the chances are that most citizens will consider the proposal on the basis of its merits rather than simply reacting according to the condition of their liver that day.

It is always well to remember that you are responsible for an *area*. You plan for an *area*. In order to stimulate citizen interest and secure action on your plans you must show your plans in terms of *area*. The common denominator of all these steps is maps.

What sort of maps do you have to start with in your town? It shouldn't be too difficult to find out. If your planning commission has been operating for awhile it surely has a number of maps available. But if it is just getting started, it might be quite another story.

It is amazing how some communities stumble along without even rudimentary map coverage of the town. I remember one town where an old Negro, long unable to do a day's work, was nearly ninety years

old and still carried on the payroll of the water and sewer department because no one else knew where the pipes were laid under the ground. Wherever trouble developed or it was necessary to tap in a new line, they would pick up Uncle Sim and take him out to the job. He would look up and down the street and reminisce a few minutes and, indicating a particular spot, suggest that they dig there, because as best he could recollect, that's about where the pipe was laid about the year after Teddy Roosevelt ran on the Bull Moose ticket.

If you don't find any maps, it's not too difficult to get started on a decent base map. Perhaps your town has been covered by the U. S. Geological survey so that the street pattern of the town would show up on one of the quadrangle topographic maps. This can be helpful to a draftsman in making a map which at least shows the established streets running in the right directions.

Again, a town of your size ought to be covered by the Sanborn map people who make maps for use by the insurance companies across the country. You can ask the leading fire insurance man in town and he should be able to tell you.

Of course, you'd check with the city engineer, if there is one, or

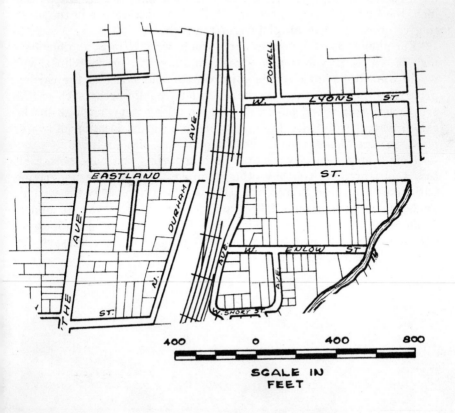

with the man who's in charge of the streets. If you still haven't got what you want, you might check with the State Highway Department and with the railroads and get what they have that applies to your town.

If you have to have your own map drafted, a recent air photograph of the town could be of great help. If your planning commission has a reasonable budget, it might be worth your while to have one of the aerial mapping companies "fly" the town. You'd be assured of having an up-to-date picture, not only of where the streets are, but what buildings are located where. There are a great many other things that you can learn from the study of such photographs or from the photographs put together into a mosaic. Also, a display of air photographs covering the town is almost a sure-fire device to catch the interest of citizens, and it is then easy to tell them what you are doing and to find out from them what they would like the planning for their town to include.

In any case, you'll need a base map which shows the streets for the whole town, and fairly accurate as to location, direction and width. If your base map is being drafted or reproduced, you may wish to have copies at, say, 400 ft. equals one inch and 800 ft. equals one inch, the former to show greater detail when necessary and the other to give an easier over-all picture of the town.

For numerous uses, you probably would want to have another base map to which, in addition to streets and streams or shorelines, you would want to have added the approximate boundaries of the various properties including the lines between lots, public areas such as the courthouse square and parks, and major utility items such as the location of railroads with their stations and yards, location of water plant, sewage disposal plant, electric plant and similar items.

Now that you have your base map materials you have gotten off to a real start, for you have the recorded layout of the underlying pattern of your city. You have a base on which to portray the various kinds of data you should collect and which will give you an understanding of the whole community. You will use your base maps again and again in your planning work, and maps will be necessary for presenting your finished plans.

V

BASIC DATA

Now to be perfectly honest about it, Mr. Commissioner, do you *really* know where the people live in your town? Do you know where the children live that attend your schools? Do you know where people work? Do you know which lands are used for industrial purposes and what lands are available to a new industry which might come along and want to locate in your town? Do you know which streets carry the heaviest traffic and where the bottlenecks are all over town? Of course, you know where *you* live and where you work and what streets you ordinarily travel and which streets you avoid, either because they are in poor condition or because it takes too long to get through them. But as far as a working knowledge of the whole city on these and other counts, it's a safe bet that your understanding could be improved upon.

So let's begin to think about getting some of these facts down on paper, preferably in map form.

One of the things that you will use time after time in your planning work will be land use data. There's nothing mysterious about getting this information, but it will take a little time and hard work for somebody. I would suggest that you start out (or have your staff do it — and we'll discuss staff in another chapter) with your base map at the 400 scale, the one which shows the lot lines. Simply travel the streets and record on the map, lot by lot, what the land is used for. In doing this field work it is very convenient to have a few colored pencils and simply to indicate on the map the various land uses by color. Light yellow is a good color to use on those lots that are occupied by separate dwelling houses. A distinctly darker yellow or orange makes a good color to show where the apartment houses are. A good bright red color may be used to show neighborhood grocery stores and drug stores, filling stations and similar outlying neighborhood commercial establishments. A darker red will indicate all businesses in the central business district. Green is a good color for parks, school grounds and other public areas (probably including cemeteries). And one or two shades of purple will help you show the location of industrial plants and grounds and to differentiate between them if you wish. When you've finished the map, be sure to (1) put a date on it; (2) record the color key directly on the map; and (3) keep it. You can make copies of the map, including black and white copies for economical reproduction, but you will certainly find that original map a valuable one throughout the years in showing what has happened

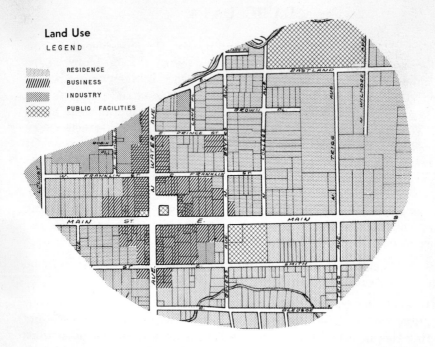

Land Use

LEGEND

▦ RESIDENCE
▧ BUSINESS
▨ INDUSTRY
▨ PUBLIC FACILITIES

to your town in terms of changes of land use since you started on your assignment.

Repeatedly you'll be wanting to know where the people live in your town. Since it's not too big a town, it will be possible to put dots on a copy of your base map, either one dot per person or one dot per family or one dot per ten people, according to your needs and the complexities of the situation. In larger cities and in cases of high density (large numbers of people per block), it may be too much of a task to actually canvass the town, plotting the location of the people. In that case, you may have to depend on census figures for small districts and record the population on that basis. Nevertheless, it is quite important for you to know where the people live because people mean traffic, people need stores, people need schools, and people are served by the water system and the sewers.

Where do the school children live? In some instances you might even want to know where the pre-school children are. Chances are that if you display a helpful attitude, rather than acting like an eccentric do-gooder or a condescending big shot, the school people can supply you with the names and addresses of children in the various grades so that those can be located on the map, and if they are

18

sufficiently excited about the proposition they may even make a special effort to get the information for you.

Now there are some other basic data that you ought to have and which may or may not be susceptible to showing directly on maps. One of the things that you should know is how the people in your community make their living. Both relatively and absolutely, just how important is manufacturing in your town in terms of number of

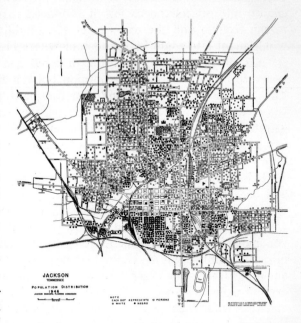

people employed? How important is trade? Do you have a university or major hospital center or major tourist attraction, and if so, to what extent does the economy of your community depend on these? Or is your community the headquarters for the state government or a major federal project? Is it the home office of a major insurance company, or is it simply the trading center and shipping point for the surrounding agricultural area? In any case, be sure you know what makes the economic wheels go round in your community because you will want to take that into account in your planning.

Incidentally, it would be a fine idea and a great help to you in your work if you had some idea as to the kind of town your town should be in future years. It's true that most towns should be diversified towns with a reasonable balance between industrial employment and trade and service occupations, and space should be provided in the land use plan so that these various types of activities can be accommodated. But it's those special needs that arise in special kinds of communities that take special attention. Take, for example, Gatlinburg, Tennessee, or Miami Beach, Florida. Both are attractive resort communities which would be much less attractive as resorts and would lose business if a large or dirty industry were to be located in their midst. Again, some towns look toward a distinct industrial future. There, the planning program should address itself vigorously to the task of protecting at least certain strategic industrial sites against encroachment by a scattering of houses. After all, when land has been cut up into miscellaneous lots it is indeed rare that industry will go to the trouble and the expense of reassembling those lands when a whole plant site could be found somewhere else.

As you pursue this question of what kind of a town you want yours to be, form your own opinion but don't depend on it entirely. Talk it over with the remainder of the planning commission and get the ideas of a number of your citizens, too. After all, it's their town as much as it is yours, and you'd be surprised sometimes at what you can learn simply by giving folks a chance to talk and express their views and ambitions.

I don't mean that you shouldn't do some thinking and exploring and dreaming on your own. Incidentally, if you take along some of your maps and keep in mind the other information that you have, you'll probably be surprised at how different the town looks now as you move around and look at it carefully. One local planning commission member got so excited along about this stage that he went out and hired a small airplane and had the pilot fly him around and around over the town so he could see it more completely and better visualize what constructive action could be taken. He saw many things that day, but one thing that he saw particularly clearly was how people from one section of the town almost *had* to go through the center of town to get to another section. He realized as never before that this was a cause of downtown congestion as well as a steady drain on the economy of the community because of the wasted time and the wasted vehicle miles consumed so unnecessarily. He visualized a circumferential major street which, like the tire of a wheel, would connect the spokes at their outer end. With a little engineering advice and after consulting a topographic map (yes, you should have one of those for your town, too), a location was decided upon for his wide new boulevard. It was incorporated into the major street plan and within a couple of years through the application of subdivision regulations all but some 4,000 feet of the entire route had been dedicated for public use without the land costing a penny of the city's funds. But I'm getting ahead of my story.

By the time you have brought together the various maps and other data that I have outlined several months will have passed. They will have been interesting months because it's ten to one that you will have learned a great deal about your town and probably will build up considerable enthusiasm about making it a better town.

But don't just go on studying and thinking, either by yourself or in simple communing with fellow commission members. You aren't in the position of the researcher delving deeper and deeper into pure science. You are a public official, potentially a very important man in local government, and you are dealing with things that touch the lives of all the people in your community. You are dealing both with public lands and public projects and with the lands and activities of private industries, businesses and individuals. To do the best job in the long run, you are going to have to have citizens and officials alike aware of you, looking to you for guidance and bringing to you statements of their problems and expressions of their aspirations. There probably was a nice little write-up in the paper at the time that the planning commission was established or when you were appointed commissioner. But don't be mistaken. Most folks have forgotten that by now. It's time that you began to use what you know in rendering miscellaneous services to them, which services will be so sound and the results so beneficial that they will be favorably inclined toward your commission and toward planning even though they may not be entirely sure just what planning encompasses.

VI

FIRST SERVICES

While you're getting on with the development of your comprehensive plan, keep your eyes open for opportunities to advise or to serve even though they may be small instances. If nothing else occurs to you, take a look at the base map again and examine the street names. Is there a real system to the street naming, and are the names sufficiently different and sufficiently clear so that there could be no confusion between them?

In one town that I know, a home was almost completely destroyed by fire because the man at the fire station thought the excited party on the telephone gave an address on Fort Street when actually the fire had broken out at that address on Fourth Street which was located on the other side of town. If these street names hadn't sounded alike, the fire engine would have gone directly to the fire and it probably would have been brought under control with very little damage. So look again and see if your town has several streets with the same name but with different endings such as Elm Street. Elm

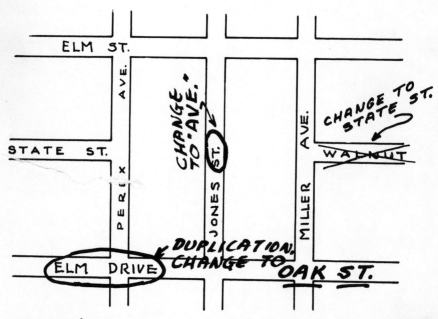

Avenue, Elm Lane and Elm Road, Elm Drive and Elm Parkway. If so, that is bad and it ought to be changed because confusion regarding which ending should be used for which street can happen

so easily and can cause anything from a failure to deliver a Christmas card to possible clouding of the title to property.

Again, are there streets running through town which bear different names in different places? If so, that ought to be rectified.

You see, I am simply suggesting that street naming is a field of activity in which the planning commission can become interested and if a need for name changes and clarification is found, the planning commission should prepare a street naming plan for the city. After ample explanation of the need for the changes, and with adequate public information, the planning commission can present its map with the proper names to the city with the recommendation that an ordinance be passed making these street names official and providing that as new streets are opened up which are extension of existing named streets, the names shall be applied throughout the length of such street. A simple ordinance provision to the effect that existing street names cannot be duplicated simply be changing the suffix will go a long way toward avoiding headaches in the future. If there is a need for this sort of thing in your town and if you do your job well, you'd be surprised how many enthusiastic supporters you can have for your planning program as a result of a few minor services like this. While some citizens will resist any change, the postmaster and the merchants as well as most of the citizens will give you a good round of applause because by this simple step you have made it easier for them to deliver their goods or find their people or direct the fire engine.

By the way, while you were checking on the street names what did you find out regarding property numbering? How do the numbers run around your place? Do you know for sure what your house number is, and are your neighbors on each side numbered harmoniously with your property? How about the folks who live directly behind you fronting on the other street? If your number is 609, is their number 608 or 610, or is it something absurd like 2117? If you find that there is no orderly system of numbering extending to properties in all sections of the city, there is a little item which your commission may well wish to study.

A good system of property numbering will have as its beginning two intersecting base lines ordinarily located along prominent routes and intersecting at a prominent point such as the public square. Or the numbering may begin at the river or waterfront. Roughly paralleling these base lines and at regular intervals there should be shown on your map a series of grid lines which will mark the beginning of each new series of numbers. For example, as Elm Street runs east from the base line, the first block would be numbered 101, 102, 103, etc., with odd numbers on one side of the street and even numbers on the other and carrying on until the grid line is reached whereupon the numbering would begin over again with 201, 202, etc. Such a system once properly established can be expanded indefinitely, harmoniously and accurately numbering all of the property in the community as the community grows.

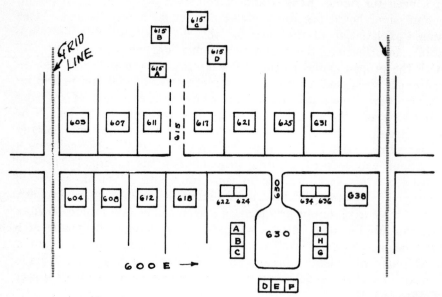

In setting up such a system remember that the numbers should be assigned on the basis of intervals of lot frontage and not assigned simply to the existing buildings. Otherwise, when a large lot is subdivided and a second house built, there will be no number left over for the new house. The property numbering system can be shown on a map and described by a text which the city may see fit to adopt officially and make effective by ordinance.

Now, mind you, street naming and property numbering may not need this kind of attention in your town and if there is no need to change, there is certainly no point in changing for change's sake. Perhaps your town needs other service items more urgently, so your planning commission should look about it and find similar items on which it can render a service to the community.

As you are establishing the place of the planning commission in the community by the rendering of services such as these and through taking official actions, do not lose sight of the unique job and the basic job, that of over-all planning for your community. Continue your work on your land use plan and your program of services to various parts of the city-to-be.

Remember also that the planning commission was established *not* because someone wanted PLANS *per se*, but because someone wanted ACTION, informed action. Never forget that the planners need not take the action, but they should produce plans so obviously workable that action follows by the city, the county, the school board, by the service clubs, individuals and citizens' groups.

This action by others will not come about in a vacuum. Someone must be sold on the idea. Who you set about to sell will depend to some degree on the action to be taken. If the action involves very broad and basic public policy, then it may be necessary to sell an entire citizenry in order to have an informed electorate that will express itself at the polls. On more technical matters — well, for example, whoever heard of holding a referendum on the question of whether the old Main Street bridge is still safe? —the city officials should be guided on that by the advice of competent engineers.

So, be democratic in your planning work and keep the people informed. But on individual items, don't hesitate to single out the man or group that can take action, and do a job of selling your plans and the need for their being carried out.

VII

YOU AND YOUR STAFF

By this time I suspect that you'll agree that you've got a big job ahead of you, that there's a lot of work to be done and that if you do the job right you are going to be in business for a long time. I don't mean that you will necessarily covet continued service in this non-paying position, but rather that as your community grows and changes, the citizens will continue to look to you for guidance if your work is sound.

Yes, this is a non-paying job and you have to make a living. You can't arbitrarily short-change your business or your family and try to do this whole job yourself. The community shouldn't expect you to. You should have some help in the way of paid staff and while circumstances may vary as affecting the source and size of the staff, nevertheless, there are some pretty definite standards for what you may expect of the staff and what the staff may expect of you. But first, let's talk about getting some staff assistance.

Any sort of staff help will cost some money and you should have some money to spend for staff and in meeting other expenses in connection with your program. You can realistically say to the city fathers that if they expect you to contribute your time and work to the best of your ability and to serve with a full measure of integrity, the least that they could expect to do is to supply you with some money to meet legitimate expenses of the planning commission.

In some small communities the expenses are not very great by virtue of having part-time assistance from somebody in city government — maybe he's the city engineer or a man in the city engineer's office. Maybe he's the building inspector or he might be any of a number of other people, provided two things: first, he has interest and ability, and second, it is clearly understood by him and his administrative superior that a specified proportion of his time is to be spent *under planning commission supervision.*

If your town happens to be located in certain of the states you could draw on a central agency for varying degrees of technical assistance. The program in Tenessee, for example, is very well developed (but terribly undermanned) by which the State Planning Commission maintains several regional offices staffed with technically trained men whose services are available to local planning commissions upon nominal payments to the agency by the cities. In this way a sort of cadre of trained, qualified talent is made available to individual cities, each on a part-time basis and at a cost to that city far less than would be involved in hiring a man of similar qualifications to serve each city separately. This system may be worth looking into if you have such a state agency with a real interest and if yours is one of a number of towns where, at least in the initial state, it appears impractical to establish your own technical staff. A program similar to Tennessee's has been in effect in Alabama for a number of years, and Kentucky, Virginia, Rhode Island and Pennsylvania instituted such programs more recently. Undoubtedly still others will initiate programs of local planning assistance under the stimulus of new federal programs.

Some towns have followed the device of appropriating a pot of money and hiring a consultant to come in and make a Master Plan. Many towns have thus "bought" master plans all done up in attractive packages and some of them have pointed the way to real community development. We might say that if such a master plan is used and modified to fit changing conditions, it is fine. But if there has been little public 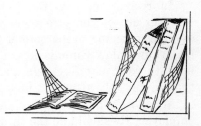 participation in drawing up one of these attractive packages, there is probably little knowledge regarding its content and little interest in carrying it out. It may turn out to be a high price to pay in order to have something to glance at admiringly and to file away until your successors hire another outside firm to come and make another master plan. I should add, however, that consultants are often very important and valuable, particularly where specialists are called in to make special studies or perform specialized tasks which are beyond the general competence of the resident staff.

Undoubtedly the best course is to have your own staff consisting of or headed by a person trained in city planning. By teaming up with him and having the public constantly available in a state of mutual confidence, you can then produce and administer the finest plan that can be drawn up. You can also make every citizen realize what it will mean to him if it is carried out.

Now let's think a little bit about your relations to your staff. If you are in the position of hiring a staff rather than calling for services from an existing city employee or an existing state agency, how should you go about it? Well, if you don't know any professionally-trained city planners who you know are competent and with whom you know you would like to work, perhaps the best thing to do is get in touch with a professional organization like the American Society of Planning Officials or the American Institute of Planners or your state planning and development agency, if you have one that is really interested in planning. Or perhaps your state university or a technical school in your state has a department of planning and, particularly if your budget is small, they can recommend to you someone who has completed his training in the field or is about to. With the vast awakening of interest in official planning programs across the country, there are plenty of jobs open to good men, so you'd better be fairly realistic in the salary offered. Otherwise you may get a second-rate man and you don't go around deliberately hiring the second best lawyer or a cut-rate doctor or a cheap man as superintendent of production in your manufacturing plant. In city planning, as well as in those fields, it pays to get a good man.

In recruiting, *you,* the Commissioner, should hire the planner, whether or not you step aside and let the mayor or the city manager or your director of personnel make the official announcement. You and your fellow commissioners are the ones who are going to team up with your planning man and you ought to insist that he be put on the payroll only after you have recommended that action.

When he is on the payroll, he is under your supervision. He is your employee. He should do the things that you tell him to do or he should get out. Chances are if he's a good man he will get out if you attempt to pervert the planning process for personal gain to yourself or favored members of the community at the expense of the general public, because good men don't have to work under those circumstances. Good planners will recognize all of the people of the city or region as their ultimate clients.

At the same time, you should be willing and anxious to listen to his recommendations and his evaluation of situations. You might even tell him where your program stands at the moment and ask him to suggest to you a program of studies and action covering, say, the next twelve months. He should be able to do this, and by the time of your next meeting, he will have something to offer. You will have something to offer, too, as an outgrowth of your knowledge of the community, your estimates of its needs, and your sense of what is of interest to the public. Between you, you should be able to lay out a vital and realistic program.

You will advance your program if you'll help him willingly and in a number of ways. You will want to introduce him to a number of people in the community and make those introductions in a favorable light so that there will be a basis for friendship and communication. Among those to whom you introduce him will be people who know a great deal about the community or people who have a great voice in community affairs. He should know the people who are responsible for changes and growth of the community, such as the people who operate the basic industries, people in the Chamber of Commerce, and people who lay out new subdivisions and build homes.

Visit his office from time to time and let him know that you are constructively interested. However, don't expect to make his office your headquarters and don't expect him to be your individual "boy." He's got a job to do, he's a professional man and you should give him every opportunity to do his job.

You can be soundly critical of him in meetings of the commission and its staff. If you find that he has too much of a tendency to deplore conditions as they exist — if his attitude is that of condescendingly endeavoring to "make a silk purse out of a sow's ear" that you call a community, feel at liberty to remind him pointedly that he took a job in the community and that he, like you, should be willing to work constructively on the situation. If you find that he is inclined to make off-hand recommendations for action on just anything that looks hot, bring him down to earth. Precipitate recommendations are poor substitutes for not planning, since it gets the same results in the same way. Hasty decisions either on his part or on your part made when the fuse on the local dynamite burns short too often uproots what was accomplished yesterday and plants seeds of trouble and expense for tomorrow. If you find that he persists in engaging in a dreamy sort of fourth dimension of wishful weaving of vision unrelated to the realities of the situation, you'd better let him go and use the money to improve your garbage collection.

At the same time, don't just challenge him for challenging's sake. Don't devil him just because he's a newcomer. You can stay out of that category and still raise penetrating, honest questions about his proposals and ask for proof to back up his findings when you feel that there's real cause for doing so.

But above all, do your criticizing and winnowing of the results of his work in conferences of commission and staff. Be sure that when you are going into a public meeting on an item of some importance that the stand of the planning commission has been enunciated. Nothing will give your critics more joy than to be able to point with derision at a split between you and your staff in public meeting. If there is a difference of opinion beforehand, hear him out. Agree with him if he's sound, and if you feel you must disagree with him, put all your reasons on the table and show him exactly why the commission's attitude is going to be thus and so. If you are speaking from realities of a situation and you feel that the realities demand something other than the ideal solution and if you tell him honestly why you are going to have to vote that way, he will keep his respect for you and work just as hard on other projects, giving you the benefit of his technical training and judgment.

Finally, leave him out of partisan politics. You can reasonably expect him to vote in elections, for every alert citizen should expect to do that. But if you have anything at all to say about it, don't ask him to work for your favorite candidate at election time and try to preserve him from being put in that position by others. His should be regarded as a non-partisan technical position and he should be allowed to conduct himself in such a manner. He should wish to conduct himself in such a manner so that regardless of changes in city administration, his work and yours can go on without interruption and without prejudice.

Now what should you except of him?

You have every reason to expect of your professional staff employee or employees that he (or they) should be morally straight, should be responsible to the extent that appropriate office hours are kept and equipment is properly handled without somebody needing to check up all the time.

You can certainly expect him to be accurate. In making a land use map, for example, he should not get sloppy or confused to the extent that he shows a particular lot devoted to industrial uses when it actually has a good residence located on it.

You can expect and insist on professional conduct. Your man has accepted professional employment and he should be personally presentable and should realize that Hollywood celebrities are about the only people in the American scene who can call themselves professional and at the same time indulge in making a spectacle of themselves in public.

You have a right to know how much technical training your man has and how much actual experience you are getting for the money you are paying. Then you should expect him to bring the full force of his training and experience to bear in doing the job to which you set him.

You have a right to expect that persons accepting employment with you are willing to accept the existing policies and will conduct themselves in a manner reflecting their allegiance to and belief in the wisdom and feasibility of the policies and program as of the time of joining the organization. This may mean that on some occasions the employee will deliberately have to subordinate his conflicting opinions. It should not mean that he is prohibited from professional discussion with colleagues and supervisors at appropriate times and places in an effort to do all that he can in an honorable manner to amend and influence the policies of the organization with which he is associated. If it ever becomes necessary, you should speak quite frankly on the subject that to remain on the payroll of an organization and undermine that organization by impugning its policies and program before outsiders is unforgivable and intolerable.

You can expect of your man that he willingly, intelligently and aggressively become acquainted with your area of jurisdiction, its people, their problems and their peculiarities. If he comes from another state or region he should try especially hard to make himself a part of the community. He should adapt his choice of words and his manner of speaking insofar as possible to the manners prevailing in the community in order not to divert attention from his thoughts by the peculiarities of his manner of speaking or his choice of words.

You should expect of him a reasonable sense of timing. This is exceedingly important in dealing with the general public and their elected representatives. Just as surely as umbrellas and overshoes sell better on a rainy day, so there are some projects or planning proposals which will sell under certain circumstances and which would be bitterly opposed or utterly ignored under other circumstances.

Your man should have a sense of humor. If he doesn't have one or if it isn't fully developed, help him to cultivate it. Without a sense of humor he is likely to find fault and to quarrel with his colleagues and his employer. A good sense of humor will go a long way in cementing agreeable relationships with the official planning commission and with the citizenry of the community in which the man is working. It will also help him to achieve a measure of contentment and of domestic tranquility when applied to the community in which he is living and the housing facilities which he finds available. If he allows things like these to get under his skin, he can ruin himself in the eyes of many and jeopardize your program.

When you get a good man, try to hold on to him. He can be many times more valuable after he has been on the job for awhile than he can be during the first few months of his employment.

Personally, between the imagination and vigor of inexperienced but properly trained youth or the ripeness of experience of a sedentary mature person whose *primary* objective is to secure a permanent berth, I would unhesitatingly choose youth. I say this because it's practical to be an idealist in planning. You must be moved by the reasons why things *can* be done and *should* be done and not by the reasons why they cannot be done.

So, choose your staff resources carefully. Let them know that you're the boss. Encourage them to turn in a professional performance for you. Reach your conclusions and establish your policies in executive session rather than argue your differences in public. Team up with your staff to the fullest in behalf of the big and important job which is to be done.

VIII

YOUR MAJOR STREET PLAN

One of the items that should be given consideration fairly early in the program is the drawing up of a major street plan for adoption by the commission. It is entirely within the province of the commission to draw up and adopt such a street plan on its own motion and it should do so for its own guidance, even though it may not feel that the plan is sufficiently final or sufficiently complete to give it wide publicity as "the last word."

A major street plan for a city includes a skeleton framework of streets which, from the standpoint of carrying traffic, are of regional importance. They carry highway traffic through the city. Such through routes will be supplemented by major access or connecting streets to serve the various sections of the city or carry heavy traffic movement within the city.

Of great utility in developing a major street plan will be your base maps on which plans may be sketched and also your maps of land use and population distribution for reference and information purposes.

These maps alone will not be enough to do the job right. You will need some other basic information including the tracing on your

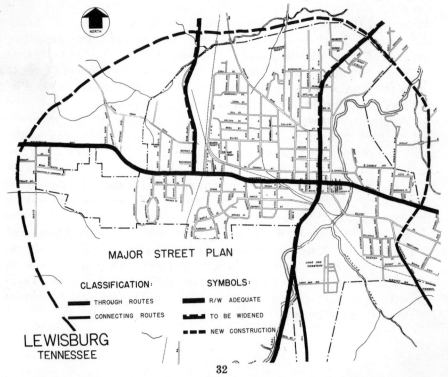

MAJOR STREET PLAN

CLASSIFICATION:

━━━ THROUGH ROUTES
─── CONNECTING ROUTES

SYMBOLS:

━━━ R/W ADEQUATE
━┅━ TO BE WIDENED
▪▪▪ NEW CONSTRUCTION

LEWISBURG
TENNESSEE

base map of the routes now followed by major highways passing through the city, together with notations regarding the width of the streets involved and the adequacy of such streets to carry the present and prospective traffic. You will especially want to note inadequacies, bottlenecks, instances of poor alignment, steep grades if any, and other bars to the smooth and safe movement of traffic which may seem pertinent.

You will also want to review, tentatively at least, the adequacy of services rendered by non-highway streets serving the various areas constituting origins and termini of major traffic movement. These will include residential sections, major concentrations of industrial employment and principal shopping areas.

You will also want to check with your state highway department and your city engineer regarding highway construction work that may be in prospect and take any such proposed improvement into account in your evaluation of the major street situation. In this connection you will want to inquire of the state highway department regarding general policies on further highway improvement in your area, particularly as to how they would regard local plans — whether they would likely regard such plans as valid expressions of local interest which, if feasible from the standpoint of engineering, they would be willing to consider on their merits in new construction.

As you talk with the state highway people you may be able to get a far better audience than an ordinary "pressure" delegation seeking special favors through wanted construction. Three significant viewpoints should be brought to their attention.

First, you can assure them that when you have drawn a plan for major streets in your town that you will then be in a position to offer them an official expression of how the people in your community want the highways to go. This will give them a sound basis on which to act and not be so subject to criticism for what may be characterized as "high-handed" tactics if the highway people presume to make the final decisions themselves without consulting local opinion.

Secondly, you can point out that if a genuinely cooperative relationship can be established between the local planning commission and the highway department, the local planning commission can know where it would be feasible to undertake new construction or to effect relocation in the predictable future. With that knowledge, it will be possible, through the administration of subdivision regulations (which we will take up in the next chapter), to obtain a great deal of the necessary right of way, adequate in width and correct in location by dedication for highway purposes through lands not yet subdivided and at great savings to the public purse. I suppose that there is no highway department which feels that it has sufficient funds to do all of the work that it would like to do in its attempt to bring roads in its state up to the standards that it would like to achieve. The prospect of accomplishing difficult and expensive projects with less friction and less money is almost automatically appealing to most highway departments.

Thirdly, you can point out to the highway department that almost without exception their control ends at the right of way stakes marking the boundaries of the public property on which the highway is built. You can point out to them that once the highway is built, especially on a "normal" right of way in or near an urban area, that that travelway is likely to become so hazardous and so congested as to be outmoded for the purpose of handling through traffic far before the day when a good modern pavement would be so broken up or worn out as to become useless. You can point out to them that with proper cooperative relationships between the highway department and the local planning commission, provisions can be written into the local zoning ordinance to require set-backs at stipulated distances from the center line or from the right of way line, and that through local zoning, formulas may be established by which off-street parking shall be provided in connection with all new businesses. Thus when business grows up along the new highways or highways to be constructed in the future, the planning commission, through foresighted action, can virtually eliminate the necessity for on-street parking and can minimize the hazards associated with access to and egress from the highway, thus preserving it for the purpose for which it was built, namely the movement of traffic.

With this kind of logic, these offers of assistance, and proposals for protection to the highway investment, there should be little question about the state highway department indicating its willingness to cooperate with you, first, in assisting you as you draft your major street plan; and, second, in following through on policy and performance, doing its part in the construction of a system for the movement of traffic that will benefit the entire community.

You are now in a much better position to give more specific study to the actual laying out of your major street plan. If your city has a traffic engineer, make use of him. If there is no such specific individual, then surely there is someone in the police department or in the city engineer's office who keeps a finger on traffic conditions, who places stop lights, who marks the channels for traffic movement in the street and who does similar work in the community. He should be a source of valuable advice and will no doubt welcome the opportunity of working with you and your staff in the development of a major street plan.

But in drawing your major street plan do not confine your deliberations to present day traffic counts, to present day street widths, or to present bearing strength of bridges that may appear along the way. Look boldly to the future and introduce a liberal amount of vision and foresight before coming to your conclusions. I recall so well when some years ago a major expressway was proposed swinging southward along the eastern side of Manhattan Island, there were those who opposed its construction. As part of their stated basis for opposition, they cited traffic counts purporting to show that very little traffic moved in that general direction. Their conclusion was that there was no justification for introducing a great traffic-carrying artery as was proposed. Others felt differently and, admitting that the traffic did not move along the precise alignment proposed for the expressway, pointed at the same time to the intolerably congested conditions along the routes that were then open for the movement of traffic. They pointed to the improved conditions which would follow the relieving of some of that traffic, including greater safety on those streets and the better setting for business operations once the through traffic was removed. This was a case where vision prevailed over narrow use of statistics and to the demonstrable public benefit.

On a much smaller scale but still vital to his community, one planning commission member in a relatively small town took note of the fact that there were large residential areas from which people moved daily into the center of town in order that they might travel out again either to employment in certain industries, to employment in a Veterans' hospital on the outskirts of the town or into the state capitol some 30 miles away. In the evening the same passage through the center of town occurred. Morning and evening this relatively small town had a real rush hour causing severe congestion with all its ramifying effects in the center of the town. It was his conclusion that the advance planning and ultimate construction of a couple of miles of connecting route terminating at a major federal highway near the city limits would permit much of this traffic movement to take place in the outskirts of the town with much less loss of time, energy and money to the persons directly involved and also render great relief to the downtown area. This stretch of new major street could be accomplished at only a fraction of the cost of appreciable widening in the downtown area, and the idea caught on readily when brought to the attention of the citizens in the community. I wish I could coin a word that would precisely characterize this kind of imagination applied to the planning process.

You haven't forgotten your land use plan in this process, I hope, because how else will you be able to estimate the needs for major streets into various parts of the city of the future? Your land use plan will show residential areas as yet unbuilt upon, but when you have

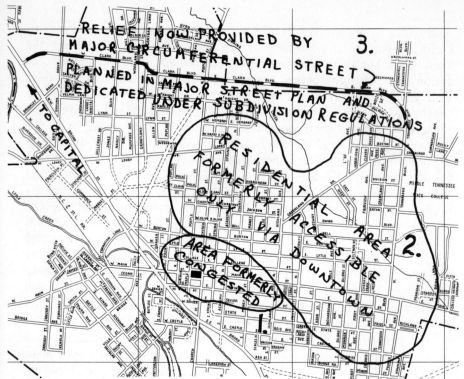

delineated those areas you have a basis for at least general computations regarding the probable population and, in turn, some indication of the volumes of traffic that will have to be handled by major streets connecting those portions of the community with other areas. Your land use plan will also show areas possible of future industrial development, and your major street plan should anticipate some arterials reaching those areas to facilitate the handling of people and materials to and from probable origins and destinations.

In your final recording of your major street plan at this stage, you may well wish to consider the presentation of chosen routes in colors by function, such as green for through routes, red for connecting routes, and perhaps blue for other routes giving access to particular points. You may well wish also to indicate by solid lines those existing routes whose location and width appear to be reasonably adequate, dashed line for new locations and by some other symbol places where widening is needed or special construction is required.

For your own guidance and for that of the staff, it is well to draw up a brief text to accompany the map which will record your thinking regarding the needs and functions of each route or part of the street plan, and such related observations as may be pertinent for future reference. Such text will serve as a guide and a reminder, and when it comes time to present a formal comprehensive plan to the city government and the general public you will find that the availability of such text will greatly simplify the preparation of such report.

At some point along the line you may wish to consciously relate your tentative efforts at a major street plan to the regional road system surrounding your city in order to be abundantly sure that there is adequate coordination between the two. It would be obviously foolish to plan a major street that would end in a cow pasture at the city limits, when by minor reorientation it could connect with and handle traffic from a highway leading in from the next town.

Even though you may not immediately publish your major street plan, you are at least now in a position of looking at street paving projects, at bridge building proposals and any other actions which may be suggested having material impact on the street system and doing so from a community-wide point of view. You are beginning now to see the community as a whole and can advise accordingly while many of your acquaintances will still be seeing a paving job only as a means to improving the surface of a street within certain blocks or perhaps evaluating same in relation to votes or personal convenience rather than community needs.

If by this time the persons in charge of streets or the local legislative body are not approaching you for advice on street projects, you might well (tactfully at first) suggest to them that you could be of help. Take them into your confidence and once again convince them that the *planning* approach is capable of orienting the details of community construction and administration toward the greater good of the entire community.

IX

ON THE SUBDIVISION OF LAND

Did you ever stop to think that about the most permanent feature of a community is the way the land is divided into parcels? Sometime when you're down that way, check in at the library and see if they have some old histories of your town or happen to have some old maps of how the town looked a century or more ago, if it has been there that long. If you can find such documents, it may be somewhat of a surprise to you that the streets and alleys shown in the downtown area are like those that are familiar to you today and to what extent the same lots that you now know show up on the old map. Old photos will show how the buildings have changed, but the lots and streets stay on.

Persons come and go, live and die, grow up and marry off and otherwise move in and out of an individual house. If your town is an old one, the house you are thinking about probably replaces an earlier house, where the same process went on. But regardless of how many houses may have been erected in succession on the same site, the chances are the lot and the street it fronts on are still there.

Consider your downtown traffic headache. It does you no real good now to wistfully say something about the short-sightedness of the town's founding fathers, and how much better it would be if they had laid out the downtown streets twice as wide. You're stuck with the streets as they were laid out unless you take some really drastic and expensive action and widen them.

Now let's think about values and living conditions. There are some sections of your town where there are nice old residences, but if they are situated on spacious lots and located decently back from the street they are still good places to live and maintain a high sales value.

In contrast, think about the worst sections of your town. It is probable that the worst of your slums are made up of miserable shacks packed closely together on lots measuring only twenty, twenty-five, or thirty feet in width and fronting on narrow, inadequate and jogging streets. Now think it over, how much of the difference in the two areas can be traced back to the way the land was laid out in the first place? The contrast is more than a coincidence. As you look at the bad areas, take yourself firmly in hand and resolve not to let it happen again.

It generally lies within the province of the local planning commission to regulate the subdivision of land within its area of jurisdiction. Your state enabling legislation generally will convey to you fairly broad powers so that you may specify the minimum width of lots, establish the widths of streets, provide for building lines or set-back lines and specify the extent to which the developer shall make physical improvements in connection with his lots. Check your legislation to see exactly what your powers are and also what prerequisites must be met, if any. In Tennessee, for example, it is required that the major street plan be adopted as a prerequisite to the establishment of municipal subdivision regulations.

You will wish to review the various portions of your area of jurisdiction which are as yet in acreage tracts and not subdivided for residential or small commercial uses. You will do well to think about which of those areas, if any, will never be feasible for service by sewers. These are the areas which for residential occupancy must then turn to septic tanks for sewage disposal purposes. While soil conditions will have a great bearing on the minimum size disposal field required for satisfactory septic tank operation, it is generally true that lot sizes in such areas will have to be kept fairly large or unsatisfactory and unsanitary conditions will occur.

An inquiry to your county health department will probably yield advice on this matter. With that information, you can arrive at decisions regarding minimum lot sizes that you will permit in those areas unsewerable or not in prospect of being served by sewers in the predictable future.

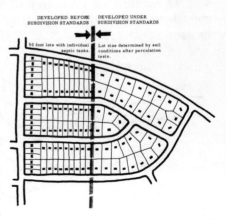

Turning then to the remaining areas, you will want to arrive at decisions regarding what in your community constitutes minimum lot dimensions for decent living. I will not pretend to tell you what those dimensions are, for the standards will vary considerably in various sections of the country and particularly with the type of housing and mode of living prevalent in various communities. The folks in the Philadelphia and Baltimore areas with row houses apparently are able to adapt their manner of living to narrower lots than folks would wish in Indianapolis, Nashville, or St. Louis, where when you live outside of multi-storied apartment buildings you live in single-family detached dwellings which benefit greatly by being on an adequate lot. Remember that in the whole process of regulating the subdivision of land you are establishing minimum standards, and if anyone wishes to develop lots that are larger or streets that are wider, encourage him to do so for he will be raising the general average of conditions in the community.

Remembering that FHA standards will generally call for 50 ft. lots as a minimum in established subdivisions and 60 ft. widths in subdivisions to be laid out, you might consider those figures as a starting place. As far as lot depth is concerned, you know yourself that some lots are too shallow for adequate living space while others are unnecessarily deep. A lot 60 ft. in width by 125 ft. in depth will afford a reasonably good setting for a small home, although more generous setting should be provided when possible, especially in connection with larger homes. In any case, establish standards for lot size for both sewerable and unsewerable areas and note them for incorporation into your body of published regulations.

You may wish to require in your regulations that in areas designed for business usage alleys of specified widths, at least adequate for two trucks to pass, be laid out and dedicated. You may wish to frankly discourage the establishment of alleys in purely residential areas, for alleys have been omitted in many successful residential subdivisions in recent years.

You will wish to provide for minimum street widths. A fifty foot street in an area that is purely residential and which street will serve only as access to a relatively limited number of houses is generally considered adequate. Never drop to 40 ft. except in the case of cul de sacs.

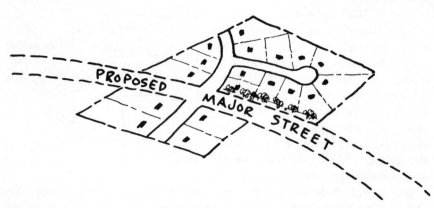

You will write into your regulations certain provisions for wider streets where, in the process of land subdivision, a portion of the major street plan is involved. Your regulations should provide that the new streets should join with other segments of the major streets which may be in existence, and be named in accordance with the established system and as a continuation of the existing streets.

You will also want to set standards for maximum grades and vertical curves, especially if yours is a hilly area, and you will want to specify the maximum degree of curvature which will be allowed in the streets.

Your enabling legislation probably will allow you considerable latitude regarding the extent to which you may require that streets be graded and improved, the extent to which sidewalks shall be laid and the extent to which underground utilities shall be installed, all by the subdivider and at his expense. Now he will cry on your shoulder and say that it will run the cost of his lots up to put in those improvements. To be sure it will, but generally speaking it is much better to do it this way beforehand than it is to allow a scattering of houses to be built on inadequate streets and then either improve the street by the assessment of abutting properties or by burdening the entire community with a long-term bond issue to finance the capital investment in making these improvements.

The community has a real interest in the establishment of set-back lines so that no buildings will be erected closer to the street than may have been specified. Actually, the set-back lines properly provided and appearing on the plat will enhance the value of the lots in the eyes of prospective buyers to a very marked degree.

You will want surveys of the lots to be accurate and shown on an accurate map. Therefore, you will want to specify that a competent engineer or surveyor be employed on the job. You will also want to be sure, in behalf of the buyers of the lots, that boundaries and corners can be accurately relocated in the future. To assure this, you may require monuments to be set in connection with every subdivision and their location be recorded on the plat map as a starting place for future surveys or resurveys.

You will want to be sure that the conditions and standards that you adopt will be met and that the very best job possible be done to adapt each new subdivision to the topography on which it is located and to secure maximum coordination with surrounding lands. Therefore, you will want to bring these items all together into a document known as Subdivision Regulations which will set forth these standards and also the procedure for subdividers to follow in obtaining the approval of the planning commission. Normally this will include the submission to the planning commission of the preliminary sketch of the area proposed to be subdivided, showing the proposed layout and when the planning commission has reviewed this sketch and has noted that standards for lot sizes, street widths, etc., have been complied with, the subdivider is given the go-ahead to do his final plat and stake it out on the ground if he wishes. After subdivision regulations are in effect, the subdivider cannot file his plat with the county register nor can he proceed with the sale of lots

THE
PRELIMINARY PLAT
SHALL SHOW:

Name, location, owner and
designer.

Date, north point and graphic
scale

Location of property lines,
roads, existing utilities, etc.

Present zoning classification

Names of adjoining properties

Proposed utility system

Names of new streets

Dimensions, lot lines and
building setbacks

Location of proposed culverts

Contours at 5' intervals

Acreage of land subdivided

Location sketch map.
See sample at end of regulations.

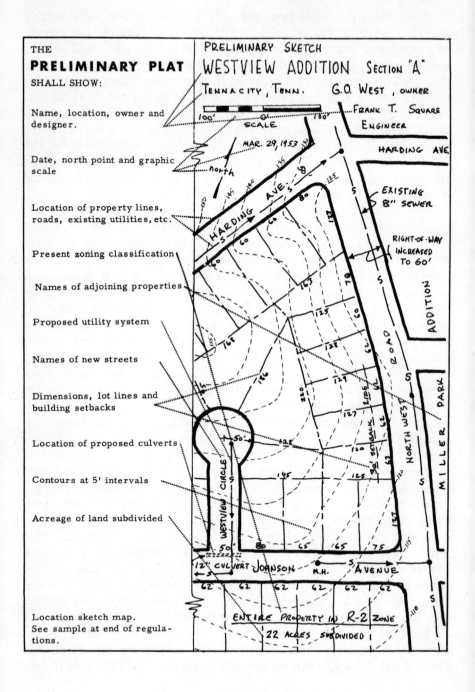

PRELIMINARY SKETCH
WESTVIEW ADDITION SECTION "A"
TENNA CITY, TENN.   G.O. WEST, OWNER
FRANK T. SQUARE
ENGINEER
SCALE
100'   0   180'
MAR. 29, 1953
north
HARDING AVE.
EXISTING
8" SEWER
RIGHT-OF-WAY
INCREASED
TO 60'
ADDITION
NORTH WEST ROAD
MILLER PARK
WESTVIEW CIRCLE
SETBACK LINE
12" CULVERT JOHNSON   M.H.   AVENUE
ENTIRE PROPERTY IN R-2 ZONE
22 ACRES SUBDIVIDED

42

THE
FINAL PLAT

SHALL SHOW:

Streets, lots, setback lines,
lot numbers, etc.

Sufficient engineering data to
reproduce any line on the
ground.

Dimensions, angles, and
bearings.

Monuments

Names of adjoining properties

Date, title, name and location
of subdivision

Graphic scale and true north
point

Location sketch map and
certificates as required - see
forms.

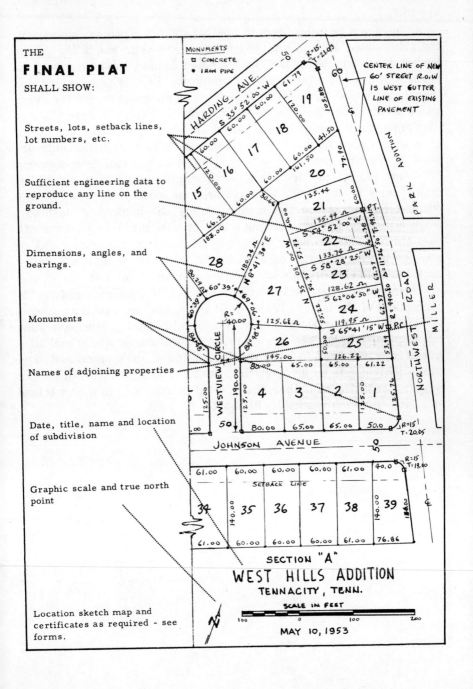

MONUMENTS
□ CONCRETE
● IRON PIPE

CENTER LINE OF NEW
60' STREET R.O.W
IS WEST GUTTER
LINE OF EXISTING
PAVEMENT

HARDING AVE.

SECTION "A"
WEST HILLS ADDITION
TENNACITY, TENN.
SCALE IN FEET
MAY 10, 1953

in any new subdivision without having submitted his plat to and obtained approval from the planning commission. Such approval is always granted when the standards set by the planning commission are met.

So now you're in business in another field, for you are overseeing the subdivision of land and you have within your hands the power to direct this process which, as we noted earlier, leaves its mark so permanently on the face of the community. In this process you can greatly raise the standards of your town as an environment for living and a location in which to invest in property. You can save the city vast amounts of money over a period of years by securing dedication of needed rights of way and by being sure that improvements are made at the time that land is opened up. Also you can, over a period of a few years, (usually it's a surprisingly short time) get all or major parts of the rights of way for your system of major streets without having to use tax money to buy the land. And normally, when a man finds that a major street or new highway location will pass through his property if he will dedicate an adequate right of way, he is glad to do so because in the long run he gets his money back handsomely through the enhanced value of his lots.

Incidentally, most states will permit you to require a reasonable percentage of the land to be set aside for public uses, such as schools or neighborhood parks, and with this in mind, and if you have your school plan in hand, you can oftentimes secure adequate school sites where they will need to be in the future and at little or no cost. The wise subdivider is happy over the situation, because after all he can sell his lots for more if they bear a good relationship to a new school or a site on which a school will shortly be built.

X

LET'S LOOK AT YOUR SCHOOLS

Sooner or later you and your colleagues are going to become interested in the schools. You should, for they are an important consumer of local financial resources as well as important institutions serving the people of the community.

I couldn't predict just how you will first become involved in the school situation. In some communities there is no particular crisis affecting schools, and the planning commission simply takes up the general subject of schools as it comes to it in the planning process. In other communities circumstances develop which force earlier attention to schools by the planning commission. In most American communities, several very powerful forces keep bringing schools to the attention of the public as well as public bodies. The postwar acceleration of birth rate is being felt in the schools with the number of school pupils outrunning the available space in all but the exceptional communities which are either declining in population or already have fostered a fairly adequate and far-sighted school construction program.

In one community in which I have been interested, additional school space was needed. The school board let it be generally known that they were going to build a new building and that it would be located on a half a city block which the city happened to own near the center of town. The city planning commission offered to make some studies relative to the school needs, and the school board replied, in essence, that it could not prevent the planning commission from making the study, but that it would be useless for they were going to build the new school on that property and thus avoid the additional expense of buying land.

The planning commission had advanced sufficiently in its studies that it had a land use plan, it had a major street plan, it had its subdivision regulations in effect, it knew where the most buildable land lay, it knew the direction in which the town was growing, it knew where the population was at that time, and it knew where the school children lived. It also had some very definite opinions regarding the areas in which new residential construction would take place, which, of course, are the same areas from which future school children would be issuing each morning. Ignoring the rebuff by the school board, the planning commission took it from there.

The plotting of known data on maps revealed to a very striking degree the fact that the proposed site was well removed from

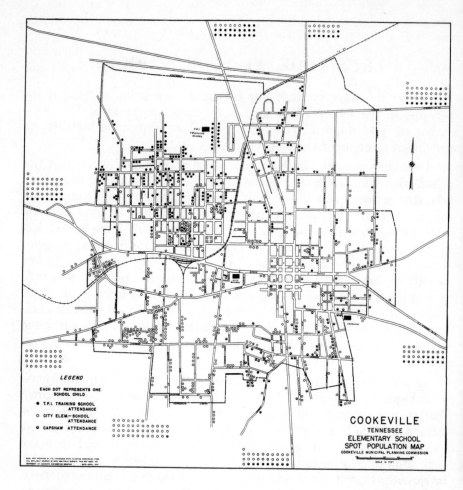

LEGEND

EACH DOT REPRESENTS ONE
SCHOOL CHILD

● T.P.I. TRAINING SCHOOL
   ATTENDANCE
○ CITY ELEM.—SCHOOL
   ATTENDANCE
◔ CAPSHAW ATTENDANCE

COOKEVILLE
TENNESSEE
ELEMENTARY SCHOOL
SPOT POPULATION MAP
COOKEVILLE MUNICIPAL PLANNING COMMISSION

SCALE IN FEET

anything like the center of the school population and that it was well removed from areas of prospective student residence. Also the area surrounding the city's land was rapidly becoming commercialized and, therefore, less used for residential purposes. This, coupled with the fact that the population remaining in the area surrounding the site was an aging population and not a source of school children tended to highlight the undesirability of the school board's plan.

Where, then, should the school construction take place? By taking what was known and estimated regarding present and future school population and applying to that knowledge a few principles such as NOT locating a school site on a major highway but rather as a center for a residential neighborhood, tentative general areas were sketched on maps. Site inspection followed at a convenient time, as did discussions regarding the cost of the land. The probable ultimate size of the school was estimated and a site was outlined which would have an acreage-enrollment ratio of at least equal to the standards recommended by the State Department of Education.

When the planning commission brought together its findings and conclusions and this information — shall we say — "leaked" out, the general public was quick to see the logic of the planning commission's proposal. The school board rapidly reversed itself and announced its intention to follow the planning commission's proposal.

As a result, a tract of 40 acres was purchased for $32,000, which will give adequate space for the school in a proper setting of open, attractive grounds and ample play space. It may even be possible to sell off a tier of lots along one side and these sales may retire the capital investment. In any case, the city is already ahead in dollars, for the downtown lot was traded for a building worth $75,000 plus $10,000 cash. The city collects $600 a month rent off the building. These figures may seem small to some people, but they are not inconsequential to a city whose annual budget is less than a half million dollars.

Subdivision of land and new residential construction was tremendously stimulated in the section of town related to the new school site and, together with a scattering of tuition-paying students from the unincorporated area, an adequate enrollment was available from the time the school was opened.

Things may not break in your town in just the same way so as to afford your commission the opportunity of making such a definite contribution to school planning. Nevertheless, your commission should make its study of the schools and plans for future school sites when the need arises or whenever the planning program has progressed to the stage of school studies, whichever be the earlier. If need arises, rise to the occasion and make a contribution. Don't say you have nothing. You probably will have more information and a better point of view than anyone else, so use it.

The foregoing illustration embodies many of the fundamental steps which you can well follow in modified form as necessary in the school studies you undertake. Presumably you will be on better terms with the school board than existed in this town at the beginning of their study, and you will want to maintain a helpful and cooperative relationship with the school board if that is at all possible. It is almost certain that they or specialists in their system are in possession of much of the data that you will need. There is no point in expending your energy or running the hazards of confusion which might follow your separate collection of data such as pupil distribution, if the existing data are sound and are available.

For this and for other studies you will want data regarding the population history and future trends of population estimates.

You probably will wish to personally inspect the existing schools in order to satisfy yourself regarding their condition, for needed replacements or expansions should be as much a part of your plan for schools as are the new schools to be built. Now it is quite one thing to go out and pleasantly visit the schools and come away with some sort of favorable or unfavorable impression. It is quite another thing, however, to look over each school with a sort of score sheet and to put down your findings for comparative purposes and future reference. Your score sheet might well include spaces for quantitative or qualitative notations on items such as size of site in acres, condition of playground, age of building, construction materials and condition of building, number of classrooms, number of other rooms, auditorium seating capacity, library, cafeteria, heating equipment, water supply, toilet facilities and data such as grades taught, number of teachers, enrollment, and average daily attendance. On the basis of data such as these you can certainly put a finger on those schools which need attention most, whether that attention be in the direction of abandonment, reconstruction, enlargement, addition to site or whatever.

To recommendations on these items you, better than anyone else, can add the picture of future needs, both as to magnitude and location, and since you have arrived at these findings on the basis of defensible data and map materials, you can amply document and substantiate your findings.

You can then probably obtain for the city some of the lands that may be required as outlined in the chapter on subdivision regulations. Encourage the advance acquisition of sites indicated by your plans. By such action you can minimize expense and disruption to development already under way, and you will have a far better chance of picking the best suited sites and securing adequate acreage for your future schools.

XI

FOR THE RECREATION OF YOUR PEOPLE

Our founding forefathers placed a great deal of emphasis on "life, liberty and the pursuit of happiness." I wonder sometimes why so many orators repeat these famous words and then promptly turn their attention to a discourse on "liberty" or "life," and fail to pinpoint attention to either the importance or the magnitude of the public interest in the third inalienable right, the pursuit of happiness.

Perhaps this lack of emphasis on facilities for the constructive pursuit of happiness is a carry over from the days gone by when there were relatively few people in this country and there was lots of space in which those few could indulge their simple pleasures. My aged father has remarked that his nearest approach to an organized sport in his early days was the gathering together of several boys from nearby farms and engaging in a contest of seeing who could travel farthest without touching the ground. Each would climb a slim young hickory tree to the point where he could bend it over far enough to catch the next one and, climbing it, repeat the process. If all present-day Americans spend their leisure time only in the process of climbing and bending hickory trees, the hickory trees by now would be indeed a sorry lot.

Speaking of lots (the other kind, of course), those are those small patches of the earth's surface on which the people in your town and every other town live and on which they cannot reasonably engage in a satisfactory and satisfying range of athletic and social activities of a recreational nature. Such activities have become much more important as we became more urbanized and as, with the shortening work day, we have more time on our hands.

To afford the advantages of recreation opportunities and to supply recreation facilities to our people, we as civilized communities are to an increasing extent undertaking community action through the channels of local government, just as we pool our efforts to supply streets, to supply schools and to supply protection of life and property.

In a good community there are a variety of public recreation facilities. There are those little spots with diminutive equipment occupying nooks in residential areas that are sometimes descriptively referred to as Tot Lots. Again, and more widely spaced, are the children's playgrounds which in many cases, and through proper advance planning, can be associated with the school properties, thus providing greater service through a more continuous use of available public lands. At still more widely spaced intervals should be

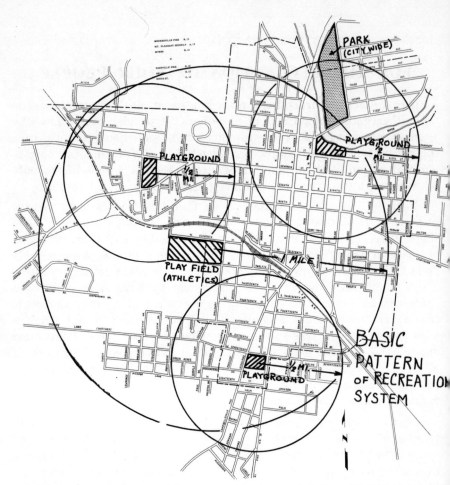

Basic Pattern of Recreation System

larger areas suitable for a wider range of activities and appealing primarily to an older group of young people — the playfields which will include some real athletic facilities. These may or may not be associated with school properties but if joint usage can be arranged, sound objectives can be achieved at lower cost than maintaining additional areas for specialized uses. Then there are the parks for resting, for strolling, for nature study, for picnicking and affording general relief to and sanctuary from the monotony of built-up city areas.

Then there are special use facilities, such as swimming pools and golf courses which are admittedly more expensive to create and operate but for which the city can legitimately collect admissions or fees from those who value them sufficiently highly to make use of them.

Again, keep in mind the indisputable but too often overlooked fact that we as a people are living longer and therefore a growing percentage of our population is older or retired persons. There is an increasing need for places where older persons can meet and engage in activities of their choosing and their liking.

In making plans for recreation in your community you will want to include provisions for most or all of the types of areas and facilities which I have mentioned. The size, spacing and number required for a balanced recreation program will vary both as to the type of facility and to the needs of the community. However, there is no escaping the fact that all are for the use of people and ought to be planned for and provided in locations bearing a sensible relationship to the people who will use them.

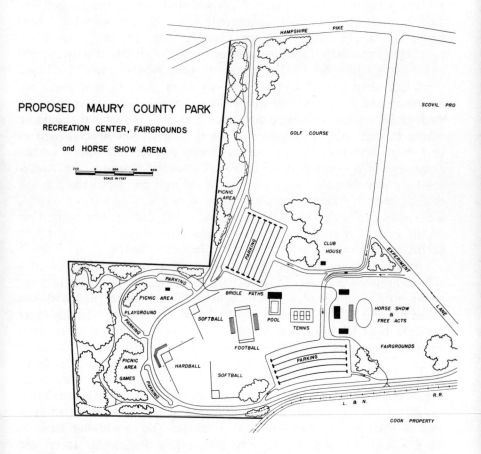

PROPOSED MAURY COUNTY PARK
RECREATION CENTER, FAIRGROUNDS
and HORSE SHOW ARENA

As a general proposition, if you do not plan ahead for them and secure the lands either by dedication (refer again to your subdivision regulation process) or by acquisition before the lands are occupied by some other use, the chances are that the land will be so expensive or the difficulties of acquisition so great that it will literally be too late to work out a really good system of recreation facilities. Of course, there are numerous instances of fine parks being established by philanthropists. Nevertheless, I would make you a small bet that in the majority of cases where a gift of land is offered to the city it will take only one look to convince you that the lands in question are so remote or so topographically unfavorable that it probably hasn't been possible to subdivide or otherwise dispose of the lands at a profit. Chances are that if the lands couldn't be used for anything else they can't very well be used as the basis for a system of parks and playgrounds, either.

So, in the interest of selecting sites for public recreation facilities, we again refer to your maps of present and future population. We refer to your land use plan; check your school plan to see what school properties might do double duty, identify large accessible areas for playfields or athletic facilities, and canvass the situation with regard to the possibilities for establishing community center type of facilities.

When sites are identified, you will want both to test them for adequacy and indicate their proper use through the drawing up for each of a site plan or development plan. This will show what should be where in each site. You may well want to get some special help at this stage, either in the way of landscape architecture talent or the assistance of a competent professional recreation person, for it certainly is true that the way a site is laid out and developed has a great deal to do with whether people will use it or not. You will, of course, make every effort to establish a cordial viewpoint toward recreation on the part of your school board, especially in relation to joint use of facilities, title to which may rest with the school board.

And here's another important point. The mere existence of facilities is no guarantee of a constructive recreation program in your community. While you're naturally more directly concerned with the selection and design of the physical properties, you should exert leadership in the direction of planning a recreation program until someone else is ready to take that over as a continuing activity. In many cities, some sort of publicly-sponsored program is already in existence, and in others some sort of program body will need to be organized. It is likely that your state either has enabling legislation providing for municipal recreation boards or commissions or at least has no statutory prohibition against them. You would not have to have a special board if your city manager is sufficiently interested and impressed to put a real program into effect, but in most cities, an interested board is the best assurance of a real recreation program, at least at the present time. In most cities such a board can be established by ordinance which can at the same time outline its powers and responsibilities.

It is probable that you will run into the question of "where will we get the money?" Well, there should be some receipts from admissions and special charges around swimming pools, golf courses and the like. But please don't anticipate that a community recreation program should be self-sustaining because if you do, you will price it out of the range of many of those who need it most. Too strong a drive for expendable receipts will tend to commercialize the whole operation.

In many cities, recreation appears in the annual municipal budget as do other beneficiaries of general fund expenditures, such as the police department, the fire department and the library. In other cities and by general permissive legislation in some states, a special recreation tax may be levied, proceeds from which shall be used for recreation purposes.

Inform yourself regarding state enabling legislation and existing ordinances, if any, and thus be prepared to discuss and exert leadership in both organizing for recreation program and the financing of recreation at the time you advance your general plan for recreation.

XII

PLANNING AND UTILITIES

You will find that in general revenue-producing utilities such as water, gas, electric, and telephone systems are not financed by means which are of direct program concern to your planning commission. Ordinarily, their operators are subject to regulation by statutory bodies, such as the state railroad and public utilities commission. Nevertheless, there are many points at which good can come from proper relationships between the planning commission and the operators of these utilities. Sewerage and the means of removal and disposition of garbage and refuse are in a somewhat different category, and planning contacts may be more frequent and even more constructive with this latter group.

We earlier touched lightly on the importance that both water and sewer people know of your planning in order that they might better choose locations for and size of mains tailored to service various areas of the city for which you are planning.

Since the water supplies or storage facilities of many communities are in the form of watersheds or storage lakes, it may be that with proper planning and coordination that recreational use can be made of these areas or water bodies. If so, a good economical solution to part of your recreation problem may be found.

The utility companies or the operating departments, if the utilities are city-owned, will be extremely interested in the work that you do in connection with subdivision regulations. If the utilities placed underground are municipally owned, the operating departments will have an immediate financial stake in the degree to which you require the developer to install such facilities prior to opening his subdivision. Whether publicly or privately owned, the utilities operators will be interested in both your plans and the subdivisions you approve in order that they may plan the extent of their expansion program and adjust the timing of that program so as to install their lines before paving is laid.

You will recall that we hinted at the desirability of omitting alleys in new residential areas. In following this procedure it is well to require, where appropriate, utility easements in the rear of lots for the installation of the pole utilities — electric and telephone — thus providing a place for them and at the same time eliminating any reason or necessity for their being installed along the residential streets. The absence of poles and wires from the streets can contribute very materially to the general appearance, livability and safety of a residential area.

Again, since the removal of sewage is usually accomplished by gravity, the sewer lines must run down hill. There may well be instances where considerable expense can be spared and future disruption avoided if, by proper coordination with those responsible for construction and operation of sewers, utility easements are provided in advance for the carrying of trunk sewer lines through properties as required by particular topographic conditions. This will apply to storm sewers as well as sanitary sewers.

As more and more communities provide for the treatment of their sewage before discharging into a stream or body of water, the matter of site for sewage treatment plant becomes more important. By proper advance coordination between the planning commission and the sewer people, at least tentative selection of treatment plant site can be made. The planning commission can, through subdivision control and otherwise, discourage the subdivision of that land or its occupancy by other uses and thus help to reserve the site for future development.

In case the community has not achieved the unimpeachable last word in the handling and disposition of garbage and refuse, the chances are that the planning commission can serve a real function in this subject area. Except under very unusual circumstances, the sanitary land fill method of garbage and refuse disposal has proven to be the best and most economical. As a first step the planning commission can focus attention on this method if it is not now in use. Secondly, the planning commission can render a valuable function in the selection of areas for such disposition. The lands used as disposal areas can as well be waste lands or low areas, and from among tracts of such description the planning commission may recommend the use of one or more particular sites. The sanitary fill method will raise the elevation of the site and with proper handling can be a means to even up the topography considerably. Areas filled in in such manner are relatively unstable for quite a while if you're thinking in terms of building heavy buildings on them after they have been filled in or leveled off. However, with proper advance planning, such areas may be considered potential park or recreation sites and what could be better than for the city to acquire waste land at a nominal figure, save money in the process of garbage and refuse disposal and end up with valuable additions in the way of park and playground lands.

As a final item regarding utilities, the planning commission can, through properly drafted and administered zoning ordinance, usually influence the design and installation of utility items such as electric substations and pumping stations so that when necessary to put them in residential areas they do not detract appreciably from their surroundings.

The direct relationships between the official planning program and utilities may seem relatively slight in comparison with some other fields, but in the aggregate the result of your activities can be of very considerable importance.

XIII

PARKING AND TRAFFIC

It's dollars to doughnuts that your town too is suffering from those familiar ills so real to so many people in so many communities — the difficulty of finding a place to park and the slowness of traffic movement. Good planning applied over a period of time can result in an appreciable improvement of the situation.

If your town is like most others, the biggest difficulty is finding a place to park downtown. Smaller similar sore spots are scattered elsewhere in the community. In the simplest sense, these are simply areas where people want to go by car and in which there just isn't enough space provided off the streets to put the cars.

It's a funny thing about parking and traffic, for everybody seems to be an expert on how the problems could be solved. Actually, in most communities there are quite a few good ideas floating around and it might pay to listen to them. You might just find some workable solutions that had not occurred to you. Some suggestions plus a little encouragement may result in private operators setting up some parking facilities with rate schedules the public would be willing to pay, and this might relieve your public problem in the matter of parking to a very considerable degree.

I recall chatting with some folks in a store in a town of about 8,000 with which I was working, and the talk turned to parking, how the curb was always parked full out in front, how customers who used to trade downtown weren't coming any more because they couldn't find a place to park, how the relationships with the farm trade had changed and how parking difficulties probably played a part in that. Talk dealt with traffic on the main drag, now slowed down both by people parking and unparking and by cars double parking either to discharge or pick up a passenger, and especially the lady who would "only be in the store a minute." So two additional traffic lanes were spoiled as far as orderly movement of traffic is concerned. One of the clerks pointed out the back window and suggested that if half the cars that tried to park in front could be encouraged to park in back that it would help the situation a lot.

That remark started a number of us to thinking. We examined our maps and air photographs. The central business area of the town was roughly three blocks by eight blocks, but as is so often the case the principal business establishments fronted on this one street. We found that a little more than half the land was covered by the stores making up the solid frontage and only a little less than half the land was virtually unencumbered. It took only a little talking to get the city fathers to commit themselves to provide an all weather surface for substantial interior block parking areas if the land would be made available. A sort of lease basis was needed so that the city would know that the land would remain available long enough to be worth surfacing. It then took only a little leadership and some patient talking to get the store people to commit themselves to allow their back yards to be used for parking by the city for a minimum of five years. The results were so successful that store owners cleaned up the back of their stores and some installed second entrances and built rear show windows in recognition of the proportion of their trade coming in from the interior of the block. A sort of competition for customers through parking was set in motion. In the outlying business areas, new stores provided convenient parking lots on the front or sides of lots. The older stores which were built up right to the sidewalk were not to be outdone, and are now advertising that they have free parking in the rear. This trend has been of inestimable value to the community.

But you should not count too heavily on such amiable and inexpensive solution or even relief to your community's parking problem. It may well be that you will need many more facts about your situation. A good start may be the securing of voluntary assistance in getting answers from downtown customers and employees on a relatively simple questionnaire form, asking a few pertinent questions: Where do you live? How did you come to town? Is your car parked on or off the street? Did you have difficulty in finding a place to park? What are you willing to pay for convenient parking space? Such data from a large sample combined with information gained from cordon counts begin to give a trustworthy picture of both the desires of persons entering the central business area and the actual number of vehicles accumulating in the business area. These totals can be measured against the actual amount of available downtown parking space, both at curbs and in off-street lots. You begin to get a realistic picture of the deficit in parking space, and where unmet needs are greatest.

Now that you have a measure of the need, what do you do about it?

One thing might be to introduce or to extend the use of parking meters in those areas where parking pressure is great and the streets are of sufficient width to be reasonably usable with curb parking allowed on one or both sides. But in the use of meters always remember this: the primary purpose of the meter should be as a device to aid the policemen in encouraging rapid turnover and thus make given space available to the very maximum number of users during a shopping day or other period of time. Meters are not primarily to collect rent for use of the street as parking space.

With the data you now have you may be better able to convince private operators that they should go into the parking business. Encourage them to keep their rates reasonable and secure a maximum amount of patronage. (After all, if cars go into the lots the pressure on your streets is reduced.)

It may be that you feel impelled to foster the development of municipal policy in the direction of municipal parking facilities. Many municipalities have provided off-street parking space and have been reasonably successful in making those facilities self-liquidating through the installation of long interval meters in such parking lots. Others have earmarked parking meter revenues for the purpose of providing off-street facilities and have found that motorists resisted the meters less when they knew for what the money would be used. Others have used the device of municipal parking authority to provide the off-street space usually purchased and developed with the proceeds of revenue bonds which, in turn, would be liquidated from parking revenues.

In any case, your planning commission should more than welcome an invitation to recommend the location of such municipal parking areas, and your parking studies should be sufficiently completed to contain ready answers.

Under many circumstances it is wise to encourage and promote the use of transit facilities which result in leaving the car at home and minimizing the parking problem.

Great benefits can be gained over a period of years by writing into the zoning ordinance appropriate parking requirements for the various districts. In this way off-street parking will be gradually accomplished in connection with residences and businesses, industries and places of amusement or assembly. There will probably be some initial protests from businesses, but when Sears Roebuck and A. & P. chain stores provide off-street parking for their customers and find that it is good business, reasonable parking requirements in connection with new establishments cannot be realistically attacked. Zoning can also require off-street loading space. Even if it's only a recessed loading dock, that big truck will be out of the way, not jackknifed across a couple of traffic lanes.

You will find that when parking is improved traffic flows will be expedited. Nevertheless there probably will remain a need for studies looking to the improvement of traffic movements, and the planning commission can make a real contribution. Study of streets where difficulties are being encountered may well uncover a number of causes of that situation and for which remedies can be found. An unnecessarily large number of stop signs or lack of coordination be-

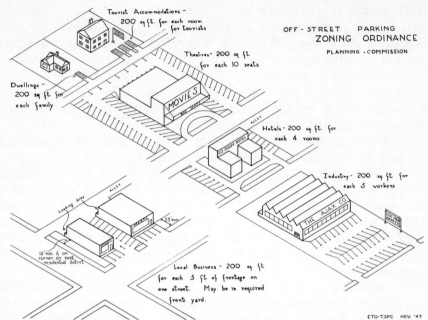

Tourist Accommodations – 200 sq. ft. for each room for tourists

Theatres – 200 sq. ft. for each 10 seats

Dwellings – 200 sq. ft. for each family

MOVIES

Hotels – 200 sq. ft. for each 4 rooms

Industry – 200 sq. ft. for each 5 workers

THE AJAX CO.

Loading Area

25 min.

15 min. if on corner or next residential district

Local Business – 200 sq. ft. for each 5 ft. of frontage on one street. May be in required front yard.

OFF - STREET PARKING
ZONING ORDINANCE
PLANNING · COMMISSION

ETO·TSPC NOV. '47

tween traffic lights may unduly slow down the movement of traffic and lead to extremes of congestion. Physical bottlenecks — narrow spots, jogs, or turns — may be uncovered and a program for their elimination can be instituted. Directional signs, one-way streets and limitation of turnings may all help in keeping the traffic moving. Channelizing of traffic in broad or complicated intersections may contribute to both the movement and safety in traffic, but a period of experimentation and observation may be necessary before the best single solution for the channelizing can be found. The traffic people or the police department probably will cooperate in the placing of temporary wooden barriers, traffic cones or the painting of lanes to find the best solution. Remember, too, that in the long haul your major street plan, if well drawn and carried out, will contribute substantially to the solution of the community's traffic problems.

XIV

A ZONING PLAN

It may seem a little strange that the discussion is only now leading around to anything approaching a thorough discourse on zoning. Actually, that's the way it should be because zoning should be looked upon as a regulatory device, aimed primarily at guiding the growth of the community according to the best plan that it is possible to devise. And if zoning is to be an instrument in effectuating a plan, it only makes sense to have the plan first and then draw up the zoning.

Oh, we've touched on zoning several times already. You remember the banker who encouraged the mayor to start a planning program because there was no zoning available to protect his house when construction started on a filling station next door. Then there was the idea of establishing formulas for off-street parking under zoning in the various business sections. There was the matter of utilities planning based on prospective land use, and you knew pretty well that the land was going to be used as indicated because you were going to zone it that way. Yes, your zoning plan should come as a latter step in comprehensive plan preparation. If you find that you've got to undertake zoning early in the life of your planning program, you had better do a lot of sketch plans in the way of land use, schools and major streets, as a guide before you actually draw your zoning map. If you do, you can proceed much more soundly and with much greater confidence that you are doing the right thing.

Now let's take a quick look and see precisely what zoning is.

Zoning is basically the regulation of the use of land. You draw a zoning plan which consists of two parts: a map and an ordinance text. After holding a public hearing and whatever other legal steps may be required by your enabling legislation, you certify the plan (both parts) to the legislative body (the city council). They have the power to adopt the plan as a penalty ordinance enforceable by use of the police power, and violations are subject to the penalties specified in the ordinance. In most states a zoning ordinance can be drawn only by the planning commission, and as a usual thing becomes effective when adopted by the legislative body. Now, let's look more closely at what should be in the plan, both on the map and in the text.

On a base map of the municipality (I told you that base map would have lots of uses), the area of jurisdiction is shown divided into districts. Basically there are three kinds of districts, industrial, commercial, and residential. Most communities exhibiting normal characteristics will need all three. Only the unnormal, such as strictly resort communities or strictly dormitory towns, can appropriately continue with less kinds of districts. Many communities will need more than just three types, and growth guidance may benefit by refinements within the major groups. Special types of districts may be established as necessary.

The size and shape of the districts will vary among themselves and from community to community. The district boundaries should be very carefully placed, reasonably reflecting existing conditions but definitely anticipating the needs of the future.

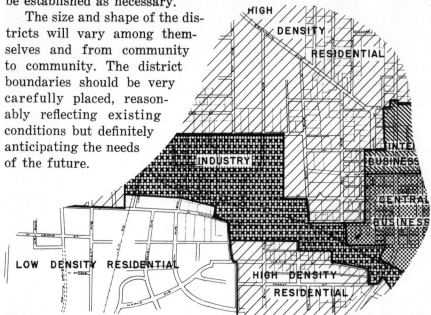

As a generalization and in a town the size of yours, there will probably be a district which is identifiable as the central business district. Here will be permitted a wide variety of commercial, professional and financial activities, probably including non-noxious service establishments.

I am sure that you enjoy the convenience of being able to make purchases and obtain some services in outlying shopping areas or neighborhood business areas. Those have a real place in the community and should be provided for on the zoning map in appropriate locations. In establishing such outlying business districts, do try your best to make *areas* of them rather than running ribbons of business zone along your major thoroughfares, thus setting the stage for traffic strangulation along those vital arteries.

You will want to establish industrial districts, for those are the workshops of the community from which much of the community's wealth originates. You may or may not wish to establish two or more types of industrial districts. In the past many communities have been calling them light industrial district and heavy industrial district. The intent may be reasonably clear, namely, that larger, noisier, dirtier or more ponderous industries would be allowed in a heavy industrial district, but that sort of terminology always invites arguments and misunderstandings as to where the division must come between industries permitted in one and not permitted in the other. Even a listing of a half hundred industries as permitted or excluded does not fully handle that situation, because no one can anticipate all future types of indutry. You simply cannot foresee what there might be about those unborn industries that would make them good neighbors or make them bad neighbors. A much better way is to establish a set of performance standards for each of the districts established and outlined on the map, and invite any industries which can measure up to those performance standards to locate in the respective districts.

In delimiting those industrial districts on the map bear in mind that industrial plants need to bring materials in and to ship products out. Therefore, carefully consider the industrial potentialities of lands bearing a favorable relationship to transporation, especially rail, navigable water and heavy duty highway and to some extent relationship to airports. Remember too, that individual industries will occupy sizeable tracts of land, and the trend in land requirements for individual industries has been definitely on the up-grade in recent years.

In laying out the industrial areas, allow sufficient land to reasonably accommodate prospective industry into the foreseeable future but don't arbitrarily over-zone and set aside for industrial purposes vast areas that probably will never be used. Consider the topography and site conditions. Set aside lands on which industry can really do a job — don't just toss the hilly, swampy or remote areas into an industrial classification to get rid of them, for the chances are that industry will never occupy undesirable sites. It will simply locate in another town if you don't have space for it.

Turning now to residential districts, you probably will need two or three types of residential districts in a town of your size. These will vary in size and location according to present conditions and estimated future needs. In one type of residential district you will want to require that houses must be built on larger lots, possibly not less than 75 ft. or 100 ft. in width and you may wish to require that those houses be set back a minimum of, say 50 ft. from the street. You probably have sections of town where those standards now apply and you will want to protect those areas from having vacant lots cut up and cracker-box houses built, lowering the neighborhood standards and hurting property values.

You probably will want a second type of residential district where the standards of minimum lot size are not set so high, where the setback requirements are not so stiff but which would still be for one-family or two-family houses.

A third category would permit the construction of apartment houses, but even though you would be allowing tall buildings and probably high density of persons per acre, you nevertheless would want to establish reasonable standards for front, side, and rear yards and otherwise plan for pleasant and wholesome living.

Aside from the three basic types of districts, special types have been introduced in a number of communities where special needs or circumstances warranted their being set apart.

Some communities have parking districts which lie as a buffer between fairly built-up business areas or industries and adjacent residential areas. Others have established flood plain districts to discourage construction in areas subject to flooding and permit only agriculture or recreation in such districts. Again, at least one town has attempted to provide itself a lasting green belt by establishing a forestry-agriculture-recreation district virtually surrounding the immediate built-up area.

You will need to explore the real circumstances, needs and prospects of your community and use your findings as a basis for decisions regarding allocating of lands to districts shown on the zoning map, and *under no circumstances* should you attempt to copy map material from another community and superimpose it on your own.

Now what about the text that will accompany the map? As a basic principle, every effort should be made to write the text simply enough for a layman to understand. After all, most of the folks who are going to be using the ordinance will be citizens without experience in planning.

The text should refer specifically to each of the types of districts shown on the map. Set forth as clearly as possible the regulations applicable in the respective district. In the central business district the text should indicate the types of land uses which would be permitted and height, bulk and area limitations on buildings. In one town about your size the planning commission couldn't make up its mind how tall they should allow buildings to be built, but when somebody pointed out that the taller the building the more people would be attracted and the more congestion would be caused in the streets, they adopted a provision that no building should be taller at any point than the horizontal distance of that point from the property line on the opposite side of the street. This has worked out pretty well, for it has allowed taller buildings along the wider streets and has avoided congestion in the narrower streets. You may want to adapt something like this for the central business district in your town.

Try your very best to work into your ordinance requirements for off-street parking in every district, including the central business district. How much parking space you can reasonably require in that area in connection with new buildings will depend to a considerable extent on how solidly your central business district is built up at the time the zoning takes effect.

In your outlying business districts, height limitations should be more severe, substantial setbacks should be required and a good formula established providing for off-street parking space in some definite ratio to floor space of stores, number of seats in theatres, and rooms commercially available to transients. It is only in this way that you can be assured that parking space will be provided as the district grows. You will also want to do some general specifying as to the kinds of uses of land to be permitted in these outlying districts — you may wish to have some filling stations, but not automobile paint shops, you might allow laundry pick-up stations and self-service launderettes, while you might not want large commercial laundry operations. And you may want to permit business signs but exclude billboards and so on down the line.

The standards for lot sizes and set-backs in the residential districts have been touched upon, but you will want to require off-street parking facilities to be provided in connection with every dwelling unit. In at least some of the residential districts, you will wish to provide for the carrying on of customary home occupations and perhaps the operation of rooming or boarding houses.

Unless you have some very experienced help in drawing your zoning ordinance or unless your staff is demonstrably competent on such matters, you may wish to secure and review zoning ordinances in effect in other communities, particularly those in your state operating under the same general enabling legislation as you are. You can learn a good deal about zoning from studying ordinances in effect elsewhere, but *write your own ordinance* and don't simply copy something from somewhere else. No two communities are the same even though they may have some characteristics in common. Because they are different, they need and should want different material in their zoning ordinances, even though both may be made operative under the same enabling legislation.

Your zoning ordinance should include provisions for a board of appeals or adjustment. Some ordinances make the planning commission the board of appeals on the theory that the planning commission which drafted the ordinance in the first place will have a better background of knowledge and vision to draw on in handling appeals that may be brought up. Other ordinances establish a separate board of appeals on the theory that a separate body would serve as a check and balance against the planning commission when it comes to administering the ordinance. Under most enabling legislation you can take your pick and you're the ones to make the decision, for after all, you will be writing the zoning ordinance.

In order to make your zoning ordinance effective, it must require that before buildings are constructed a building permit must be secured. Upon application for such permit the building inspector will review the plans of the project and will satisfy himself that the construction to be undertaken is entirely in keeping with the zoning regulations applicable to the districts in which construction is proposed. If it does not, the building permit is not issued and to proceed without such permit or in a manner not in keeping with the provisions of zoning makes the party liable to the penalties prescribed in the zoning ordinance.

In connection with proposals to occupy or in case of change of occupancy of a property, an occupancy permit is required. This is the point of control to prevent somebody starting out to build a house and then deciding to make a grocery store out of it.

As you can well see, once zoning is installed its administration becomes a continuing process. From then on, all new buildings and changes in occupancy must be handled upon appropriate permits and in keeping with the zoning regulations.

XV

OTHER PLANNING MATTERS

At no time have I pretended to undertake to give you a comprehensive course in city planning. Although some of these subjects have been discussed in some detail, nevertheless my primary objective has been to give you a basis for sizing up your powers and responsibilities as a member of a municipal planning commission and to help you to grasp the comprehensive quality of a good plan and program.

To somewhat complete this picture then, there are some areas of subject matter which ought to be brought up even though they be not much more than mentioned.

One of these is the matter of public buildings.

Let's start with your city hall. Check the situation sufficiently so that you can answer with confidence: is it adequate and is it properly located? If the answer is no, then the city hall ought to be brought in as part of your planning program.

That in itself begins to open some additional possibilities for exploration. You might ask yourself similar questions about the buildings or office space occupied by the fire department, the police department, the jail, the health department, the utilities headquarters if municipally owned, and the headquarters or the offices or laboratories of other city agencies.

Let me tell you about another community, and see if it gives you any ideas. A decade ago, interest was stirring on the subject of a new fire hall since the fire engine had been unable to get out promptly because parked cars blocked the narrow street in front of the fire hall. This simply served to highlight the inadequacies of the situation, and the mayor asked the planning commission to specially advise the city on the subject.

It so happened that the city hall amounted to little more than the clerk's office on one side of the fire hall and the police headquarters was little more than a desk in the back room alongside two iron cages which served as the jail. The town which was less than 3,000 population in 1940 was undergoing considerable growth and something needed to be done on several counts. Obviously more adequate fire headquarters situated in relation to very adequate egress was required. Larger, better and more dignified city offices and council meeting space was overdue. The headquarters of the municipally-owned electric system, including offices and meter room, were located in a slightly remodeled residence of inadequate dimensions. The city health department was not satisfactorily situated. There was no city garage, and city trucks along with electric department vehicles were taken home overnight by their drivers.

This happened to be the county seat town and one hardly need go inside the county courthouse to realize that a suitable modern building was overdue.

As a result, the planning commission reported back to the city government suggesting the desirability of planning a civic center. Described were the probable differences in cost, in convenience and in civic pride if a small-scale civic center could be established, as against the alternative of all the departmental needs being ultimately satisfied in a series of separate facilities scattered opportunistically over a considerable part of the town. The idea caught on.

But a new city hall to house all of these city functions would cost a lot of money. How could a town that size finance that sort of thing? Well, first the electric department solicited offers from local capital sources on the amount of monthly rent that would be required were these capital sources to build an electric headquarters building to reasonable specifications and lease it to the electric department on a twenty-year basis.

Contact was made with an able architect who roughed out tentative plans and cost estimates on a building which would house the city offices, power offices and the meter room, police department, fire department, jail, and space for use as city garage. These studies revealed that the payments that would be made by the power department in occupying privately built and leased facilities would, when applied to interest payments and debt retirement on a non-profit tax-free city building as designed by the architect, very nearly retire the cost of the building in twenty years. The city then took the planning commission recommendation and appropriated a few thousand dollars of general funds toward the building and financed the remainder by revenue bonds which would be retired from the rental payments by the electric department over the 20-year period. The building is now a model to other communities in that portion of the state, and the citizens are tremendously proud of it. It occupies an entire city block which had to be condemned at a stiff price, but it is located in the right place as an element of the civic center fronting the area where the new courthouse will be built, flanked by a high school and by the community's recreation center.

Of course, you may not have exactly the situation in your community, but the happenings in this smaller town illustrate the kinds of needs which may be discovered and will suggest some of the turns which may be encountered as your planning touches on the matter of public buildings.

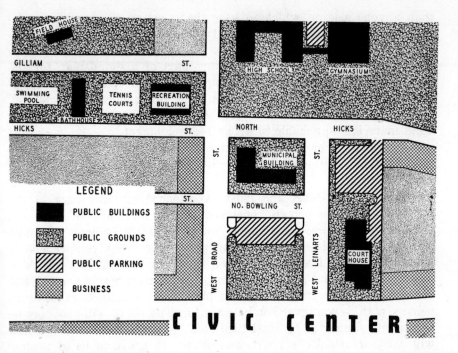

GILLIAM ST.

SWIMMING POOL · TENNIS COURTS · RECREATION BUILDING · BATHHOUSE

HICKS ST.

HIGH SCHOOL · GYMNASIUM

NORTH HICKS

MUNICIPAL BUILDING

ST. · NO. BOWLING ST.

WEST BROAD · WEST LEINARTS · COURT HOUSE

LEGEND

■ PUBLIC BUILDINGS

▨ PUBLIC GROUNDS

▧ PUBLIC PARKING

▤ BUSINESS

CIVIC CENTER

Another major field in which you probably will be interested sooner or later is that of urban redevelopment.

As noted earlier, about the most permanent thing about a community is the way the land was laid out in the first place. In almost every community the size of yours there are areas which are not only poorly laid out but which through age and deterioration have come to be true slum areas, breeders of ill health, crime, and immorality. Such areas are prodigious consumers of public finance, falling far short of paying their way through taxation.

It is rare that responsible business or the builders of good homes will see fit to try to reassemble significant portions of such areas and invest money rebuilding them to higher standards. If these festering conditions are to be removed, it is almost necessary that the city take action through its appropriate redevelopment instrumentality. Federal recognition of these conditions has resulted in the establishment of an agency and funds for assistance to local communities in redeveloping such areas.

Whether or not the planning commission takes the initial initiative in urban redevelopment it is sure to become involved, and a better job can be done if the planning commission brings an appropriate amount of leadership to the task.

Unless there is a well-established redevelopment authority in existence, it is probable that the planning commission has more data than anyone else on which to base the selection of areas for redevelopment. Then federal participation in getting the job done increasingly requires that sound plans for redeveloping the chosen site be submitted and that those plans are part of a sound plan for the entire community. This places it squarely in the planning commission's lap. So, as you work along in your program you will do well and serve your community if your data collection and plan-making build materials applicable to urban redevelopment.

There is another planning matter on which we should give a little thought. That is the matter of relationship of consulting talent to your program.

Some of the ablest and most experienced city planners in the country operate as private consultants. They maintain an office and staff, and for a fee you can employ one of these men or firms to handle almost any planning job, including preparation of a comprehensive plan. If you have the money, it's an easy way out, for you tell them what you want, and they will deliver you an attractively printed and bound ordinance, site plan, traffic plan, capital budget, or comprehensive plan — whatever you bargain for. The result will probably be adequately supported by statistical data, be written in language that will weather attacks in court, and otherwise prove to be of professional caliber.

But I wonder — is the perfect document the thing you really want, or do you want to improve your community and strengthen the practice of democracy at the same time? Reflect for a moment on your own efforts. You are working with your fellow commissioners on something bigger than just a one-shot published document. You are (or should be) working also with the elected city officials and city employees, and with citizens generally, on an *approach* to the solutions of local problems as well as finding the solutions themselves. If you do your job well, you will have benefited by ideas, suggestions, and the expressed aspirations of your fellow citizens. If you're on the job a couple of years you will find that, due to changing conditions, what appeared to be a pat solution earlier, now no longer fills the bill. The plans have to be changed in some respects to meet the new situation. To blindly follow the printed plan might be the height of folly. How much better if you, your co-workers, and your staff are able, in the light of your experience and knowledge of the situation, to make those changes and re-adapt your plans.

Now, suppose you had turned the whole job over to a consultant. What might have happened? He or his crew might have come to town, set up shop, ignored the general public, collected their data, and written you a report. You might not have known where they got their data nor how they arrived at their conclusions. Your fellow citizens might have had little chance to speak, and their wishes not reflected in the product. The newspaper notice of completion of THE PLAN would excite few, for most would have had no part in it. Having no interest and no knowledge of the matter, most citizens would not put work and enthusiasm into carrying out the plan.

I will admit that I am biased, but my bias is based on a very definite philosophy — a philosophy proved successful by practical test. I feel that turning general plan-making over to a consultant is a sad mistake. I believe that there is no substitute for the *building* of a plan as a result of continuing effort of the commission and its staff, in close cooperation with a maximum number of citizens. The plan will come to naught without popular support, and support does not come without understanding and participation.

Now don't get me wrong, I am not playing down the importance of trained professional talent in the plan-making process. But much of that talent should be in the form of regular staff. Such staff will have the benefit of knowledge of your community and its needs, even though it may not be fully proficient in some of the knottier technical aspects of planning. There's where consulting talent can often be splendidly utilized — supplementing your staff with know-how on special problems. You may wish to have a consultant periodically review your work and give you advice. But utilize him as a *consultant* in *your* planning program.

71

XVI

CAPITAL BUDGET PROGRAMMING

As knowledge of your plan-making leaks out (and you should tell the world about what you are doing), you are sure to meet those critics who will look over your best efforts and say, "Hmm, very pretty, but where are you going to get the money?" There's where the capital budget comes in.

This is a process which is characterized by various names such as Capital Budget Programming, Capital Outlay Planning, or Capital Improvement Planning. They are all synonyms for the same idea, which is essentially one of consciously balancing moneys available or which may reasonably be expected to become available against the volume of needed construction and improvements in such a way that the most needed items will be cared for first with other needs to be met in a logical planned order over a period of years. The period of years may vary, but most cities choose to make their plans for a period of six years — the present fiscal year, plus five years into the future. Capital budgets made for less than this period often suffer from the difficulty from being too close to immediate problems, while plans for more than six years tend too often to get into the realm of fancy rather than of concrete program.

How do you go about it? Well, the first step naturally is to look over the financial position of the city, noting its income by sources and its outgo by objects. The sources tapped should be evaluated against the background of revenue sources legally available to the city in order to identify any equitable sources of additional revenue not now being utilized. I think you will find that your city enjoys two things in common with most other cities. First, the city is generally pictured as being broke or at least hard up. Second, it is not using all the sources of revenue legally available to it. In addition to reviewing the sources you may have reason to give some inspection to the adequacy and completeness of collection of revenues, including a review of the extent to which assessments are made and equalized in the property tax field.

Your second major step is to determine the categories and amounts of outgo, both in operations and in debt service and retirement. At this step, it is likely that you can spot a number of places where the city can save money. One town I know had a truly handsome balance in a checking account in the bank, drawing no interest while it had outstanding indebtedness on certain equipment on which it made monthly payments, plus 6% on the unpaid balance. The prompt payment of this indebtedness with part of the non-interest-earning money saved the town those high interest payments and made a real difference in the town's financial position. Opportunities for other efficiencies, either in personnel, purchasing, supplies or equipment may be similarly cited as a result of study.

So the first two steps should give you the financial picture, also a basis for action to improve the city's income and minimize its outgo and thus tend to create a margin which would be available for capital improvements.

As a third step, the capital needs in the community should be brought together. Some of these will be derived from the plans developed by the planning commission. Others will be pointed out in consultation with the city manager and/or officials heading the various branches of city government. Included may well be items ranging from fire hose and police cruisers, and garbage trucks to schools, bridges, swimming pools and other recreation facilities. Rather careful estimates should be worked out for the costs of the projects or items listed, and the items should be ranked in terms of urgency.

Now, an estimate of outgo for non-capital purposes is made for each of the six years of the period, and measured against the actual or estimated income including the special charges, savings, and other improvements recommended as result of earlier study. The difference between the two, year by year, is the best basis possible for estimating the amounts of money that may be available year by year for capital improvements. By setting these totals against the expenses involved in the various projects which have been ranked according to urgency, it is possible to proceed with the scheduling of the individual projects.

The capital budget should be reviewed each year, perfected to the extent possible by substituting actual figures for previous estimates and then projecting the program an additional year into the future so that it is always reasonably long-range.

Since the power to levy taxes and appropriate funds rests with the legislative body, the capital budget will work only through such legislative body. This makes it very important to coordinate closely with that body in the process. As a practical procedure, it would be well if the planning commission inquires of the city fathers regarding their interest in such a study before undertaking it. Then keep them informed of progress. They will be interested. Tell them of the untapped revenue sources and of the concrete opportunities for saving through better fiscal management. Give the councilmen or aldermen a chance to look over your lists and ranking of projects and offer suggestions.

When the study is completed and approved by the planning commission, carry it to the legislative body for official adoption. If they demur, hesitating to bind themselves by full adoption, perhaps they will adopt it in principle and as a guide until its value has been proved to them.

Having done so, the document has many values to the legislative body. Primarily, it is their timetable for their program of local public works improvements. But the secondary uses soon loom large. If they have levied any new taxes or special charges, or revised and equalized assessments, the irate citizens can be largely pacified by showing them where the money is going and for what purpose. Again, I suppose every city government has been snared into undertaking unpremeditated actions by special interest groups who send delegations to city council meetings. From this point henceforth, such groups can be heard, then invited to inspect the capital budget. They can be shown what moneys there are, what it will take to run the city, and what improvement projects are ranked and scheduled. If their project is really worthier than those, a deliberate reranking can be done at the time of the annual restudy. If their project doesn't measure up — well, it can be disallowed for demonstrable cause, and without recriminations. The administrative branch, also knows where it's going, and can do a better job.

XVII

HOW ABOUT YOUR OUTSKIRTS?

You have the job of planning inside the city pretty well shaped up and, given a little time for your work to become really effective and to show results, a marked improvement in the city should be evident.

But did you ever stop to think that about the time your city builds up to its corporate limits and your plans will in large measure have been fulfilled, then that will be about the time that the city will extend its boundaries and annex some new territory. What kind of territory will it be able to annex when the time comes?

If the territory contiguous to but lying outside the municipality is not within any planning jurisdiction then it will be without a comprehensive plan and growth will take place in an unguided, unregulated and un-coordinated manner. Narrow streets and narrow lots may have been laid out, and poor housing built. A mixture of houses, automobile wrecking yards, filling stations, and drive-ins may even now occupy the area. When annexing tidbits like that, the city is virtually bringing in the equivalent of the areas cleaned out by urban redevelopment.

Since we know how to guide the growth within the city and regulate the use of land in the public interest, it just doesn't make sense not to do it in the growing suburban areas that surround the city. The city has a real stake in building the kind of areas it wants to annex in the future.

In some instances planning by the counties takes care of the areas outside the municipalities and those areas will be in good shape if and when annexation comes about.

But what if the county isn't interested in establishing a planning program? Well, some states have an answer for that one. In Tennessee, for example, in a situation where there is an active city planning commission and the county chooses to do nothing, it is possible under law to grant extraterritorial planning authority to the municipal planning commission with jurisdiction beginning at the city limits and extending outward not more than five miles in all directions. This has proved to be a very workable means of getting planning programs in effect in such areas before it is too late, and this is especially valuable in instances where the county does not choose to carry on.

If as a result of your interest in the surrounding areas regional powers are granted to your municipal planning commission, you can in large measure extend to such areas the same planning you have done inside the city. What I mean is this: the municipal major street plan can be extended, with roads and highways reaching across the larger area and become a fully coordinated major thoroughfare plan for the local region. In the matter of subdivision regulation, the standards inside and outside the city might well be the same unless there are obvious circumstances which would alter such an approach. It may be desirable to apply even higher standards outside the city in terms of minimum lot area. It may be entirely contrary to municipal policy to extend underground utilities into the unincorporated area. Therefore, there would be no point in requiring a subdivider to install sewers if there are no trunk lines or disposal plant into which such sewers could lead. Without sewers, one must resort to septic tanks, and larger lots should be required to supply successful disposal fields.

In the matter of schools, the approach to building a school plan would be essentially the same as in the case of the city although you would be dealing with other people and perhaps less known quantities.

Outside the city as inside you should develop at least a tentative land use plan which, as we have already mentioned, is basic to any sound efforts in the direction of a comprehensive plan.

Just as you established working relationships with the city government and its public works officials, you would establish similar relationships with the county government and its divisions because they will be the ones who will actually put plans into effect and pass your zoning ordinance or resolution before it becomes applicable to the unincorporated area. You will want to publicize your efforts, your purposes and your progress to the people in the larger community and make every effort to find common ground for thinking on the part of both the city and the suburban population.

Yes, it's adding to your responsibilities to think in terms of a local region consisting of both the city and its immediate environs. However, if there is no one else who is willing to undertake the extra work and with whom you can cooperate and coordinate, then you may have to do the job if the long-term public interest is to be served.

XVIII

PRESENTING THE COMPREHENSIVE PLAN

Throughout your work you should have maintained a maximum amount of communication with the general public and kept them informed of what you were doing and the beneficial results achieved. In this growing process there is no instrumentality which can be as helpful as the press in reaching the public and in writing for public consumption the real news of what you are doing. The press is usually quick to recognize the importance of a planning commission's work in the community and will consider its findings and recommendations as worthy of reporting. Provided, that is, the planning commission plays square with the press and does all within its power to make it easy for the press to do the reporting. If representatives of the press attend planning commission meetings, the reporters may make their own notes on the actual incidents which transpire on such occasions. You will want to fill them in on the background of some of the actions, but even the meeting reports are relatively superficial and ephemeral in comparison to the results the press can achieve in the way of public understanding. Try to convey to the press a basis for grasping the field of planning, what it can mean in community development, and the relative importance and interrelationships of the various steps in the planning process.

But in spite of public understandings gained and interim reports made to the people, there will come a time when you will want to bring the result of your studies to date altogether into one coordinated document. This will be the published Comprehensive Plan and when completed should be officially adopted by the planning commission and really should be accepted officially by the city government. Without such official action its legal status is perhaps comparable to a descriptive brochure issued by the Chamber of Commerce. Once it is officially adopted, however, it becomes the guidebook for future development. It can be amended and it can be deviated from by tangible official action by the same body which adopted it. There *should* be amendments and deviations as the years go by in order to meet changing conditions. Nevertheless, such action should be official and there should be a good and sufficient reason for each instance of such action.

In bringing the comprehensive plan together you will review and include all or most of the various specific plans that you have accomplished to date. You will want to check these plans one against the other, for you can now improve each of them, at least in clarity of presentation. You are now in a better position to highlight the interrelationships between them. Similarly, you will want to re-examine and perfect your land use plan for it may well be that some of the other plans, while generally harmonious with the early draft of a land use plan, will have provided a basis for variations in land use or will have involved facilities not specifically indicated on the original map.

You will want to summarize the physical improvements proposed and display your capital budget, especially the highlights from analysis of city finances and the scheduling of improvements — both from the standpoint of ranking according to need and from the standpoint of probable timing in the light of anticipated availability of funds.

You will want your comprehensive plan document to be attractive. If your budget is slim, even a *little bit* of color here and there will help. If your budget has flexibility at all, you may wish to secure a little help on matters of illustration or layout or on typography. You may be able to have your favorite newspaper man to scan it from the standpoint of whether the public will read it and understand it.

When it's ready to go to press, be sure to order enough copies. It certainly will not perform its function if the distribution is limited to planning commission members and a few city officials. You will want to make it available to schools, libraries, civic groups and thinking citizens. If you can possibly arrange it, run a few copies extra for swapping with other planning commissions across the country. They are just as interested in your accomplishments as you are in knowing what the other fellow is doing. You might even put a price on the publication and sell it to people outside your community and thus recoup part of the costs of publication.

In any case, you will have brought the major results of perhaps several years' effort together as a permanent document, both as a record of progress to date and as a guide for tomorrow's action.

XIX

THE CONTINUING PROGRAM

Don't just tuck your copy of the comprehensive plan under your arm (duly autographed by your colleagues on the planning commission) and go home with a feeling of — well, that's over. Maybe your period of most intensive work and greatest exertion is now past, but that comprehensive plan isn't going to be worth a thing if it simply collects dust on somebody's shelf and if nobody uses it until it is exhumed as a starting place for another comprehensive plan sometime in the future. You must see to it that your plans are thoroughly understood and appreciated by the officials who are in a position to implement them.

By now you are probably sufficiently interested that you really want to see the whole thing through. I hope you are, because that's the way the best results will be obtained.

For one thing, you have put zoning into effect and you will want to be sure that it is properly administered. You will want to be sure that building permits and occupancy permits are issued only in keeping with the terms of the zoning plan.

You will also want to keep your subdivision regulations in effect, and for them to be of any consequence whatever, the plats of areas proposed to be subdivided must be reviewed and approved by the planning commission. Approval ofttimes comes only after some real hard work with the subdivider in helping him to make the subdivision the best one possible for his land and to secure coordination of streets and services of that particular subdivision with the remaining structure of the city.

There will be changing conditions which will require your attention. You may wish to recommend amendment of the zoning ordinance from time to time, whether in the adjustment of the districts shown on the map when good and sufficient reason is brought to your attention, or you may wish to improve the ordinance text on the basis of experience, new practices and new court decisions. Perhaps the off-street parking regulations written in at the time that the ordinance was originally passed were as stringent as you could get by with at that time, but perhaps by now the idea of off-street parking under zoning has come to be generally accepted. Perhaps now there would be applause rather than objections if you revised the ordinance to require more realistic and larger amounts of parking space, at least for some districts or uses.

You will be wanting to work along on other things such as an official street map, especially if you were unable to incorporate one into your comprehensive plan. In connection with your official street map, you will want, on the basis of engineering survey, to plot future street lines outlining the area that will be necessary for street widening to carry out your major street plan. This done, new buildings will not be erected in the bed of such mapped streets except with the understanding that when the street is widened, the buildings so erected will be removed without compensation to the owner. This is being done in an increasing number of places. In Miami, Fla., for example, much progress has been made as result of one building after another being thus set back in the process of construction or reconstruction until the particular street widening project becomes financially feasible of accomplishment.

You will want to keep constantly abreast of new developments in city planning elsewhere. From the body of such experience and on the basis of precedents established, you can bring to bear those results for the benefit of your own community.

You will constantly want to provide leadership or to supplement other efforts in behalf of the economic development of your town. You might be surprised how many nationally-known industries, when seeking the best location for new plants, take into account whether the individual community has an operating planning commission and displays the benefits of good planning. Some industries, of course, have special location requirements that virtually dictate their choice of site. Those requiring a huge water supply, for example, could not possibly consider locating in your community if you have no huge water supply available. But there will be other industries that will seek the location and resources which your town has to offer. As location selection simmers down to a choice between your town and other towns, you're more likely to get the nod if yours is an attractive town, an efficient town, one offering a good range of good public services and facilities, if its zoning will provide space for industrial location and extends protection to the residential areas in which executives and workers will live. Yes, a *good* town is more attractive than a subsidy to worthwhile industry, and you can do a lot of planning on less money than is involved in many subsidies.

And you will want to encourage the expansion of your community. Your birth rate will exceed your death rate, which will mean an increase in population if they all stay there. If your town is a good place to live and your children and your friends' children can find advantageous employment, they will remain with you and make their contribution to the community after you have contributed to them their upbringing and education at public expense. Then, too, property values, business conditions and many aspects of community life are quite different in a town that is still growing as against one that is static or declining in population.

Yes, planning is a continuing process. You will find participation in it a rich experience, Mr. Commissioner. As time goes on you will recognize even more the real opportunity that official planning afforded you to make a contribution to your children and to your fellow man. The satisfaction in seeing the accomplishment of worthwhile things as a result of your foresight and efforts will give you a sense of satisfaction. You'll be proud to be called Mr. Commissioner. Yours, an unspoken personal feeling that after all, maybe you *were* the most important man in local government.